CIMA

Operational level

F1

Financial Reporting

Exam
Practice Kit

For exams from 4 November 2019 to January 2021

Fifth edition 2019

ISBN 9781 5097 2676 9
e-ISBN 9781 5097 2677 6

British Library Cataloguing-in-Publication Data
A catalogue record for this book
is available from the British Library

Published by

BPP Learning Media Ltd
BPP House, Aldine Place, 142/144 Uxbridge Road
London W12 8AA

www.bpp.com/learningmedia

Printed in the United Kingdom

Your learning materials, published by BPP
Learning Media Ltd, are printed on paper
obtained from traceable, sustainable sources.

We are grateful to the Chartered Institute of
Management Accountants for allowing us to
reproduce extracts from the CIMA exam blueprint. An
up-to-date version of the full blueprint is available at
www.cimaglobal.com/examblueprints.

BPP Learning Media is grateful to the IASB for
permission to reproduce extracts from the
International Financial Reporting Standards
including all International Accounting Standards, SIC
and IFRIC Interpretations (the Standards). The
Standards together with their accompanying
documents are issued by:

The International Accounting Standards Board (IASB)
30 Cannon Street, London, EC4M 6XH, United
Kingdom.

Email: info@ifrs.org Web: www.ifrs.org

Disclaimer: The IASB, the International Financial
Reporting Standards (IFRS) Foundation, the authors
and the publishers do not accept responsibility for
any loss caused by acting or refraining from acting
in reliance on the material in this publication,
whether such loss is caused by negligence or
otherwise to the maximum extent permitted by law.

Contents

Question and Answer index   iv

Using your BPP Exam Practice Kit   v

Examination structure   vi

How to pass   ix

Questions and answers

Questions   3

Answers   63

Practice mock

Questions   103

Answers   123

Question and Answer index

Objective test questions	Page number	
	Question	**Answer**
1 Regulatory environment and corporate governance	3	63
2 The Conceptual Framework	7	64
3 Non-current assets	10	67
4 Leases	13	70
5 Other accounting standards	16	72
6 Presentation of published financial statements	23	76
7 Statements of cash flows	30	81
8 General principles of taxation	34	84
9 Direct taxation	37	86
10 International and indirect taxation	42	89
11 Working capital and the operating cycle	46	91
12 Receivables, payables and inventory	50	93
13 Managing cash	55	96
Mock	103	123

Using your BPP Exam Practice Kit

One of the key criteria for achieving exam success is question practice. There is generally a direct correlation between candidates who study all topics and practise exam questions and those who are successful in their real exams. This Kit gives you ample opportunity for such practice throughout your preparations for your OT exam.

All questions in your exam are compulsory and all the component learning outcomes will be examined so you must **study the whole syllabus.** Selective studying will limit the number of questions you can answer and hence reduce your chances of passing. It is better to go into the exam knowing a reasonable amount about most of the syllabus rather than concentrating on a few topics to the exclusion of the rest.

Practising as many exam-style questions as possible will be the key to passing this exam. You must do questions under **timed conditions.**

Breadth of question coverage

Questions will cover the whole of the syllabus so you must study all the topics in the syllabus.

The weightings in the table below indicate the approximate proportion of study time you should spend on each topic, and is related to the number of questions per syllabus area in the exam.

P3 Risk Management Syllabus topics	Weighting
A. The Regulatory Environment of Financial Reporting	10%
B. Financial Statements	45%
C. Principles of Taxation	20%
D. Managing Cash and Working Capital	25%
	100%

Examination structure

The Objective Test exam

Pass mark	70%
Format	Computer-based assessment
Duration	90 minutes
Number of questions	60
Marking	No partial marking – each question marked correct or incorrect All questions carry the same weighting (ie same marks)
Weighting	As per syllabus areas All representative task statements from the examination blueprint will be covered
Question Types	Multiple choice Multiple response Drag and drop Gap fill Hot spot
Booking availability	On demand
Results	Immediate

What the examiner means

The table below has been prepared by CIMA to further help you interpret the syllabus and learning outcomes and the meaning of questions.

You will see that there are five skills levels you may be expected to demonstrate, ranging from Remembering and Understanding to Evaluation. CIMA Certificate subjects only use levels 1 to 3, but in CIMA's Professional qualification the entire hierarchy will be used.

Skills level		Verbs used	Definition
Level 5	**Evaluation** *The examination or assessment of problems, and use of judgment to draw conclusions*	Advise	Counsel, inform or notify
		Assess	Evaluate or estimate the nature, ability or quality of
		Evaluate	Appraise or assess the value of
		Recommend	Propose a course of action
		Review	Assess and evaluate in order, to change if necessary
		Select	Choose an option or course of action after consideration of the alternatives

Skills level		Verbs used	Definition
Level 4	**Analysis** *The examination and study of the interrelationships of separate areas in order to identify causes and find evidence to support inferences*	Align	Arrange in an orderly way
		Analyse	Examine in detail the structure of
		Communicate	Share or exchange information
		Compare and contrast	Show the similarities and/or differences between
		Develop	Grow and expand a concept
		Discuss	Examine in detail by argument
		Examine	Inspect thoroughly
		Monitor	Observe and check the progress of
		Prioritise	Place in order of priority or sequence for action
		Produce	Create or bring into existence
Level 3	**Application** *The use or demonstration of knowledge, concepts or techniques*	Apply	Put to practical use
		Calculate	Ascertain or reckon mathematically
		Conduct	Organise and carry out
		Demonstrate	Prove with certainty or exhibit by practical means
		Determine	Ascertain or establish exactly by research or calculation
		Perform	Carry out, accomplish, or fulfil
		Prepare	Make or get ready for use
		Reconcile	Make or prove consistent/compatible
		Record	Keep a permanent account of facts, events or transactions
		Use	Apply a technique or concept

Skills level		Verbs used	Definition
Level 1/2	**Remembering and understanding** *The perception and comprehension of the significance of an area utilising knowledge gained*	Define	Give the exact meaning of
		Describe	Communicate the key features of
		Distinguish	Highlight the differences between
		Explain	Make clear or intelligible/state the meaning or purpose of
		Identify	Recognise, establish or select after consideration
		Illustrate	Use an example to describe or explain something
		List	Make a list of
		Recognise	Identify/recall
		State	Express, fully or clearly, the details/facts of
		Outline	Give a summary of
		Understand	Comprehend ideas, concepts and techniques

(CIMA exam blueprint, 2019)

How to pass

Good exam technique

The best approach to the computer-based assessment (CBA)

You're not likely to have a great deal of spare time during the CBA itself, so you must make sure you don't waste a single minute.

You should:

1   Click 'Next' for any that have long scenarios or are very complex and return to these later

2   When you reach the 60th question, use the Review Screen to return to any questions you skipped past or any you flagged for review

Here's how the tools in the exam will help you to do this in a controlled and efficient way.

The 'Next' button

What does it do? This will move you on to the next question whether or not you have completed the one you are on.

When should I use it? Use this to move through the exam on your first pass through if you encounter a question that you suspect is going to take you a long time to answer. The Review Screen (see below) will help you to return to these questions later in the exam.

The 'Flag for Review' button

What does it do? This button will turn the icon yellow and when you reach the end of the exam questions you will be told that you have flagged specific questions for review. If the exam time runs out before you have reviewed any flagged questions, they will be submitted as they are.

When should I use it? Use this when you've answered a question but you're not completely comfortable with your answer. If there is time left at the end, you can quickly come back via the Review Screen (see below), but if time runs out at least it will submit your current answer. Do not use the Flag for Review button too often or you will end up with too long a list to review at the end. Important note —studies have shown that you are usually best to stick with your first instincts!

The Review Screen

What does it do? This screen appears after you click 'Next' on the 60th question. It shows you any incomplete questions and any you have flagged for review. It allows you to jump back to specific questions **or** work through all your incomplete questions **or** work through all your flagged for review questions.

When should I use it? As soon as you've completed your first run through the exam and reached the 60th question. The very first thing to do is to work through all your incomplete questions as they will all be marked as incorrect if you don't submit an answer for these in the remaining time. Importantly, this will also help to pick up any questions you thought you'd completed but didn't answer properly (eg you only picked two answer options in a multi-response question that required three answers to be selected). After you've submitted answers for all your incomplete questions you should use the Review Screen to work through all the questions you flagged for review.

The different Objective Test question types

Passing your CBA is all about demonstrating your understanding of the technical syllabus content. You will find this easier to do if you are comfortable with the different types of Objective Test questions that you will encounter in the CBA, especially if you have a practised approach to each one.

You will find yourself continuously practising these styles of questions throughout your Objective Test programme. This way you will check and reinforce your technical knowledge at the same time as becoming more and more comfortable with your approach to each style of question.

Multiple choice

Standard multiple choice items provide four options. One option is correct and the other three are incorrect. Incorrect options will be plausible, so you should expect to have to use detailed, syllabus-specific knowledge to identify the correct answer rather than relying on common sense.

Multiple response

A multiple response item is the same as a multiple choice question, except **more than one** response is required. You will normally (but not always) be told how many options you need to select.

Drag and drop

Drag and drop questions require you to drag a 'token' onto a pre-defined area. These tokens can be images or text. This type of question is effective at testing the order of events, labelling a diagram or linking events to outcomes.

Gap fill

Gap fill (or 'fill in the blank') questions require you to type a short numerical response. You should carefully follow the instructions in the question in terms of how to type your answer – eg the correct number of decimal places.

Hot spot

These questions require you to identify an area or location on an image by clicking on it. This is commonly used to identify a specific point on a graph or diagram.

A final word on time management

Time does funny things in an exam!

Scientific studies have shown that humans have great difficulty in judging how much time has passed if they are concentrating fully on a challenging task (which your CBA should be!).

You can try this for yourself. Have a go at, say, five questions for your paper, and notice what time you start at. As soon as you finish the last question try to estimate how long it took you and then compare to your watch. The majority of us tend to underestimate how quickly time passes and this can cost you dearly in a full exam if you don't take steps to keep track of time.

So, the key thing here is to set yourself sensible milestones, and then get into the habit of regularly checking how you are doing against them:

- You need to develop an internal warning system – 'I've now spent more than three minutes on this one calculation – this is too long and I need to move on!' (less for a narrative question!)

- Keep your milestones in mind (eg approximately 30 questions done after 45 mins). If you are a distance from where you should be then adjust your pace accordingly. This usually means speeding up but can mean slowing down a bit if needs be, as you may be rushing when you don't need to and increasing the risk of making silly mistakes.

A full exam will be a mix of questions you find harder and those you find easier, and in the real CBA the order is randomised, so you could get a string of difficult questions right at the beginning of your exam. Do not be put off by this – they should be balanced later by a series of questions you find easier.

Objective test questions

1 Regulatory environment and corporate governance

1.1 Which one of the following bodies is responsible for reviewing new financial reporting issues and issuing guidance on the application of International Financial Reporting Standards?

- ⊘ International Accounting Standards Board
- ○ IFRS Foundation
- ○ IFRS Interpretations Committee
- ○ IFRS Advisory Council

✗ *Interp. committee*

1.2 Which one of the following is responsible for governance and fundraising in relation to the development of International Financial Reporting Standards?

- ○ International Accounting Standards Board
- ○ IFRS Interpretations Committee
- ⊘ IFRS Foundation Trustees ✓
- ○ IFRS Advisory Council

1.3 Which of the following provides advice to the International Accounting Standards Board (IASB) as well as informing the IASB of the implications of proposed standards for users and preparers of financial statements?

- ⊘ IFRS Advisory Council
- ○ IFRS Interpretations Committee
- ○ IFRS Foundation ✓
- ○ IFRS Foundation Trustees

1.4 Corporate governance can be best defined as:

- ⊘ A system by which companies are directed and controlled
- ○ A system of control designed to manage risk ✓
- ○ A system that allows for corrective action and penalising mismanagement
- ○ A system that ensures director accountability to shareholders and stakeholders

1.5 Which of the following would NOT be regarded as good practice for the nomination committee?

- ○ The nomination committee should consider the need to attract board members from a diversity of backgrounds.
- ⊘ The nomination committee should consist entirely of executive directors. ✓
- ○ The nomination committee should regularly review the structure, size and composition of the board.
- ○ The nomination committee should consider whether non-executive directors are spending enough time on their duties.

BPP
LEARNING
MEDIA

1.6 Which of the following is NOT an advantage of global harmonisation of accounting standards?

- ⊘ Priority given to different user groups in different countries
- ○ Easier transfer of accounting staff across national borders
- ○ Ability to comply with the requirements of overseas stock exchanges ✓
- ○ Better access to foreign investor funds

1.7 Which recommendation of the Sarbanes–Oxley Act addresses the problem of over-familiarity of the audit firm with the client?

- ○ Rotation of lead audit partner every year
- ⊘ Rotation of lead audit partner every five years ✓
- ○ Rotation of audit firms every three years
- ○ Rotation of audit firms every seven years

1.8 The setting of International Financial Reporting Standards (IFRSs) is carried out by co-operation between the IFRS Foundation, the IFRS Advisory Council and the IFRS Interpretations Committee.

Which of the following reports to the International Accounting Standards Board (IASB)?

- ○ IFRS Foundation
- ○ IFRS Advisory Council
- ⊘ IFRS Interpretations Committee ✓
- ⊘ IFRS Advisory Council and IFRS Interpretations Committee

1.9 Which THREE of the following are the responsibilities of the IFRS Foundation Trustees?

- ☐ Issuing International Financial Reporting Standards
- ☐ Approving the annual budget of the IASB ✓
- ☑ Enforcing International Financial Reporting Standards
- ☐ Reviewing the strategy of the IASB and its effectiveness ✓
- ☐ Appointing the members of the IASB, the IFRS Interpretations Committee and the IFRS Advisory Council ✓

1.10 Which THREE of the following are characteristics of a purely principles-based approach to corporate governance?

- ☑ It focuses on adherence to a single set of standards.
- ☑ It can be applied across different legal jurisdictions. ✓
- ☐ It can stress those areas where rules cannot easily be applied. ✓
- ☑ It puts the emphasis on investors making up their own minds. ✓
- ☐ It includes definite targets for companies to meet.

1.11 **Which TWO of the following are characteristics of a rules-based approach to corporate governance?**

☐ It allows companies to operate on a comply or explain basis.

☑ It emphasises measurable achievements by companies.

☐ It covers all eventualities.

☑ It can easily be applied in jurisdictions where the letter of the law is stressed.

☐ It can easily be applied across different legal jurisdictions.

1.12 **Which of these would constitute an advocacy threat?**

○ The audit firm being sued by the client

○ The audit firm and the client being sued by a third party

○ The audit firm suing the client for non-payment of fees

⊘ The audit firm giving evidence in court on behalf of the client

1.13 Safeguards can be put in place to avoid threats to independence arising from a specific engagement.

Which of these is NOT a safeguard?

○ Rotating senior assurance team personnel

○ Discussing ethical issues with those charged with governance of the client

○ Getting another firm to perform part of the engagement

⊘ Recruiting senior management for the client

1.14 A professional accountant in business may be involved in a wide variety of work.

Which of these functions will the accountant NOT be carrying out?

○ Preparing financial statements

⊘ Auditing financial statements

○ Preparing budgets and forecasts

○ Preparing the management letter provided to the auditors

1.15 **Which of the following is NOT one of the five fundamental principles of professional ethics in the Code of Ethics?**

○ Integrity

○ Objectivity

⊘ Reliability

○ Confidentiality

1.16 A professional accountant is required under the Code of Ethics to comply with five fundamental principles.

These include:

- ○ Integrity, Objectivity, Reliability
- ○ Professional competence and due care, Confidentiality, Integrity
- ○ Morality, Objectivity, Professional behaviour
- ○ Efficiency, Confidentiality, Professional competence and due care

1.17 A qualified accountant holds a number of shares in his employing company, and has become eligible for a profit-related bonus for the first time.

What type of threat could this represent to his objectivity when preparing the company's financial statements?

- ○ Self-interest
- ○ Self-review
- ○ Intimidation
- ○ Familiarity

1.18 While at a party at the weekend, you meet a client of yours who is clearly very concerned about some VAT issues. You know enough about VAT to carry out your daily work, but you are not an expert on the areas of imports and exports on which your client is asking your opinion.

What ethical issue does this situation raise?

- ○ Objectivity
- ○ Professional competence and due care
- ○ Professional behaviour
- ○ Confidentiality

1.19 **Which of the following is an advantage of a principles-based ethical code?**

- ○ It can easily be legally enforced.
- ○ It provides rules to be followed in all circumstances.
- ○ It encourages compliance by requiring a professional person to actively consider the issues.
- ○ It can be narrowly interpreted, making it easy for the professional to see whether or not the Code has been violated.

1.20 **Which of the following is NOT a circumstance where disclosure of confidential information is permitted under the Code of Ethics?**

- ○ Disclosure of information when authorised by the client
- ○ Disclosure of information to advance the interests of a new client
- ○ Disclosure of information to protect the professional interests of an accountant in a legal action
- ○ Disclosure of information when required by law

2 The *Conceptual Framework*

2.1 Which of the following is NOT true regarding the IASB's *Conceptual Framework for Financial Reporting*?

- ○ It encourages companies to present information faithfully.
- ○ It gives a framework to be followed in all circumstances when preparing and presenting a set of financial statements.
- ○ It is an accounting standard that companies have to comply with.
- ○ It is useful to existing and potential lenders in making decisions.

2.2 Which of the following is NOT an element of the financial statements as covered in the IASB's *Conceptual Framework for Financial Reporting*?

- ○ Assets
- ○ Liabilities
- ○ Profits
- ○ Equity

2.3 Which TWO of the following statements describe comparability?

- ☐ The non-cash effects of transactions should be reflected in the financial statements for the accounting period in which they occur and not in the period where any cash involved is received or paid.
- ☐ Similar items should be treated in the same way from one period to the next.
- ☐ Information must have a predictive and/or confirmatory value.
- ☐ Similar items within a single set of financial statements should be given similar accounting treatment.

2.4 Which of the following options correctly describes the status of the IASB's *Conceptual Framework for Financial Reporting*?

- ○ It carries the force of law.
- ○ Compliance ensures that a true and fair view is given.
- ○ No departures are allowed from the contents of the framework.
- ○ It provides a framework for the formulation of accounting standards.

2.5 Which THREE of the following options are advantages of the IASB's *Conceptual Framework for Financial Reporting*?

- ☐ It can suggest solutions to difficult issues whilst ensuring a consistent approach.
- ☐ It helps entities ensure that their financial statements comply with local legislation.
- ☐ It helps to reduce the scope for individual judgement and potential subjectivity.
- ☐ It demands that financial statements contain relevant information.
- ☐ It is consistent with US GAAP.

2.6 **Which TWO of the following characterise faithful representation in the IASB's** *Conceptual Framework for Financial Reporting*?

☐ Use of information that has the ability to influence decisions

☐ Information that is free from error

☐ Information that is complete

☐ Information that is capable of direct verification

2.7 **Which THREE of the following are NOT underlying assumptions from the IASB's** *Conceptual Framework for Financial Reporting*?

☐ Accrual accounting

☐ Going concern

☐ Faithful representation

☐ Relevance

2.8 **Which TWO of the following are benefits which arise from having a conceptual framework such as the IASB's** *Conceptual Framework for Financial Reporting*?

☐ The information needs of all user groups will be better served.

☐ Accounting standards will develop in a more coherent fashion.

☐ Different accounting presentations of transactions not currently covered by IAS/IFRS should reduce.

☐ The task of developing and implementing standards will become easier.

2.9 The IASB's *Conceptual Framework for Financial Reporting* requires information to be faithfully represented.

Which of the following is an aspect of faithful representation as defined in the IASB's *Conceptual Framework for Financial Reporting*?

○ Classification

○ Consistency

○ Neutrality

○ Predictive value

2.10 **Which TWO of the following are included in the purpose of the IASB's** *Conceptual Framework for Financial Reporting*?

☐ It assists those preparing financial statements in complying with local legislation.

☐ It assists those preparing financial statements in developing consistent accounting policies where an IFRS allows a choice of accounting policy.

☐ It assists the Board of the IASB in the development of future International Financial Reporting Standards and in its review of existing standards.

☐ It eliminates misleading financial statements as there are always fundamental principles to refer to.

2.11   Which TWO of the following are the fundamental qualitative characteristics of
        financial information per the IASB's *Conceptual Framework for Financial Reporting*?

        ☐   Consistency
        ☐   Understandability
        ☐   Comparability
        ☐   Reliability
        ☐   Relevance
        ☐   Faithful representation
        ☐   Predictive value

2.12   Which option best describes the purpose of financial reporting as set out in the IASB's
        Conceptual Framework for Financial Reporting?

        ○   To provide information about the reporting entity that is useful to tax authorities
        ○   To enable investors to decide whether to buy or sell shares in the entity
        ○   To provide information about the reporting entity that is useful to a variety of users
        ○   To enable financial institutions to decide whether or not to lend to the entity

2.13   Which of the following is the definition of a liability as set out in the IASB's *Conceptual
        Framework for Financial Reporting*?

        ○   A present economic resource controlled by the entity as a result of past events
        ○   Decreases in equity other than those relating to distributions to holders of equity
             claims
        ○   A present obligation of the entity to transfer an economic resource as a result of past
             events
        ○   A right that has the potential to produce economic benefits

2.14   How does the IASB's *Conceptual Framework for Financial Reporting* define a reporting
        entity?

        ○   A legal entity
        ○   A parent company and its subsidiaries
        ○   An entity that is required, or chooses, to prepare financial statements
        ○   Two or more entities not linked by a parent–subsidiary relationship

2.15   'The price that would be received to sell an asset or paid to transfer a liability, in an orderly
        transaction between market participants at the measurement date.'

        This is a definition of which measurement basis?

        ○   Historical cost
        ○   Fair value
        ○   Value in use
        ○   Current cost

3 Non-current assets

3.1 Which THREE of the following costs can be included in the total cost of producing an asset by a company for its own use?

- ☑ Directly attributable labour costs
- ☑ A reasonable proportion of indirect costs
- ☑ Interest on capital borrowed to finance production of the asset ✓
- ☐ Depreciation charges for the asset
- ☐ Ongoing maintenance charges for the asset

3.2 Which TWO of the following can be included in the calculation of the cost of a non-current asset as per IAS 16?

- ☑ For a purchased asset, expenses incidental (directly attributable) to the acquisition of the asset
- ☐ For a manufactured asset, only the direct costs of production
- ☑ For a manufactured asset, direct costs of production plus a reasonable proportion of indirect costs
- ☐ Annual maintenance costs ✓

3.3 A freehold property originally costing $100,000 has accumulated depreciation to date of $20,000. The asset is to be revalued to $130,000.

Which set of double entries is required to record the revaluation?

- ○ Dr Accumulated depreciation $20,000; Cr Revaluation surplus $20,000
- ○ Dr Revaluation surplus $50,000; Cr Accumulated depreciation $20,000, Cr Property at cost $30,000
- ○ Dr Property at cost $50,000; Cr Revaluation surplus $50,000
- ○✓ Dr Accumulated depreciation $20,000, Dr Property at cost $30,000; Cr Revaluation surplus $50,000 ✓

3.4 IAS 16 *Property, Plant and Equipment* requires non-current assets to be depreciated using:

- ○ A method that allocates the cost as fairly as possible
- ○ A method that allocates the depreciable amount as fairly as possible ◁
- ○ The straight-line method or any similar method ✗
- ○✓ The straight-line or reducing balance method

3.5 Bradley Co depreciates non-current assets at 20% per annum on a reducing balance basis. All non-current assets were purchased on 1 October 20X3. The carrying amount on 30 September 20X6 is $40,000.

What is the accumulated depreciation as on that date? Give your answer to the nearest thousand dollars.

40 000 × 100/80 = 50 000

$ 74600 ✗

3.6 Which TWO of the following non-current assets would normally require depreciation?

- ☐ Freehold land
- ☑ Freehold buildings
- ☐ Investments
- ☑ Plant and machinery ✓

3.7 Which of the following would NOT be classed as a non-current asset?

- ○ Freehold property, occupied by the entity and held for its investment potential
- ○ Freehold property, occupied by the entity and used as its head office
- ⊘ Shares in another company held as a short-term store of spare cash
- ○ A 'limited edition' delivery van used in the entity's operations ✓

3.8 Wilson has leased a building for 10 years and is setting up a new production plant.

Which of the following should NOT be capitalised as part of the cost of the production plant?

- ○ Transport costs delivering machinery to the plant
- ○ The cost of dismantling the production plant which is required at the end of the lease
- ⊘ Initial operating losses while the production plant reaches planned performance
- ○ Fees paid to engineers overseeing the installation ✓

3.9 A ship requires a safety inspection every three years as a condition of being allowed to operate. The cost of the inspection is $10,000.

How should this cost be treated in the financial statements?

- ○ Accrued for over three years and charged to maintenance expense
- ○ Provided for in advance and charged to maintenance expense
- ○ Charged in full to profit or loss when the expenditure takes place ✓
- ⊘ Capitalised and depreciated over the period to the next inspection

---

3.10 A company purchased a machine for $50,000 on 1 January 20X1. It was judged to have a five-year useful life with a residual value of $5,000. On 31 December 20X2 $15,000 was spent on an upgrade to the machine. This extended its remaining useful life to five years, with the same residual value. During 20X3, the market for the product declined and the machine was sold on 1 January 20X4 for $7,000.

What was the loss on disposal?

- ○ $31,000
- ○ $35,000
- ○ $31,600
- ○ $35,600

3.11 The components of the cost of a major item of equipment are given below.

	$
Purchase price	780,000
Import duties	117,000
Sales tax (refundable)	78,000
Site preparation costs	30,000
Installation costs	28,000
Initial operating losses before the asset reaches planned performance	50,000
Estimated cost of dismantling and removal of the asset, required to be recognised as a provision	100,000
	1,183,000

What amount may be recognised as the cost of the asset, according to IAS 16 *Property, Plant and Equipment*?

○ $956,000

○ $1,105,000

⊘ $1,055,000

○ $1,183,000

3.12 IAS 16 *Property, Plant and Equipment* requires an asset to be measured at cost on its original recognition in the financial statements.

EW used its own staff, assisted by contractors when required, to construct a new warehouse for its own use.

Which ONE of the following costs would NOT be included in attributable costs of the non-current asset?

○ Clearance of the site prior to work commencing

○ Professional surveyors' fees for managing the construction work

⊘ EW's own staff wages for time spent working on the construction

○ An allocation of EW's administration costs, based on EW staff time spent on the construction as a percentage of the total staff time

---

3.13 VBN Co purchased an asset for $10,000 on 1 April 20X2. The asset was deemed to have a ten-year useful life and no residual value and was depreciated on a straight-line basis up to 1 October 20X3, when the depreciation method was changed to 20% on a reducing balance basis.

Calculate the carrying amount of the asset at 31 March 20X6.

○ $5,440

⊘ $4,896

○ $4,096

○ $6,120

3.14 DVR Co purchased an asset for $40,000 on 1 January 20X1. At that time the asset was deemed to have a useful life of ten years and a residual value of $4,000. At 31 December 20X3 it was decided that the asset had a remaining useful life of five years. The estimate of residual value was unchanged.

Calculate the depreciation charge for the year ended 31 December 20X4 in respect of this asset.

$ 6560 ✓

Have to use residual amount again.

3.15 AGH Co purchased a building on 1 January 20X4 for $500,000 and commenced depreciating it over a 50-year useful life. On 1 January 20X6 the building was revalued to $960,000 and it was sold on 1 July 20X6 for $1,100,000.

Calculate the amount that will be credited to profit or loss as the gain on disposal.

$ 140,000 ✗

Do depreciate when year not held for sale.

4 Leases

4.1 ABZ Co leases an item of plant on 1 April 20X3. The present value of lease payments not paid at the commencement date was $15,600 and three annual instalments of $6,000 per annum are payable in arrears on 31 March each year. The interest rate implicit in the lease is 8%.

Calculate the amount that will appear under non-current liabilities in respect of this lease in the statement of financial position at 31 March 20X4.

$ 173 ✗

4.2 Which TWO of the following are TRUE as per the definition of a lease as set out in IFRS 16 *Leases*?

- ☐ The contract relates to any one of a number of assets.
- ☑ The lessee obtains the right to use an asset in exchange for consideration.
- ☐ The lessor has the right to direct the use of the asset.
- ☑ The asset cannot be substituted by the lessor. ✓

4.3 On 1 July 20X1 CBV Co entered into a contract to lease a building for ten years. It paid a deposit of $100,000 and initial direct costs were $28,000. At the end of the lease period the building will need to be decommissioned. The present value of the decommissioning costs at 1 July 20X1 was $40,000.

The present value of lease payments not paid at 1 July 20X1 was $900,000.

What was the initial measurement of the right-of-use asset?

- ○ $900,000
- ○ $1,000,000
- ○ $1,028,000 ✓
- ◉ $1,068,000

4.4 DNK Co has received a lease incentive of $50,000 on entering into a leasing contract.

How should the incentive be accounted for?

- ○ Added to the initial measurement of the right-of-use asset
- ☑ Deducted from the initial measurement of the right-of-use asset
- ○ Added to the initial measurement of the lease liability
- ○ Deducted from the initial measurement of the lease liability ✓

4.5 The initial measurement of a right-of-use asset at the commencement of the lease on 1 January 20X4 is $800,000. The lease term is six years and the useful life of the asset is eight years. Ownership is expected to be transferred at the end of the lease period.

What will be the carrying amount of the asset at 31 December 20X5?

$ 533333   ✗

4.6 On 1 April 20X7 VNG Co entered into a contract to lease an asset for four years. Instalments of $45,000 are payable in advance, with the first payment due on 1 April 20X7. The present value of the lease payments not paid at 1 April 20X7 is $118,000. The interest rate implicit in the lease is 7%.

What is the current liability in respect of the lease at 31 March 20X8?

- ○ $81,260
- ☑ $45,000
- ○ $50,688
- ○ $39,312 ✓

4.7 **Which TWO of the following transactions must be accounted for as leases in accordance with IFRS 16 *Leases*?**

- ☐ TDK Co has leased a property for $50,000 a month for 10 months.
- ☑ PYM Co has leased a machine for $3,000 a month for 18 months.
- ☐ ADV Co has leased a desktop printer for $100 per quarter for two years. ✓
- ☑ WVX Co has leased a car for $5,000 a year for four years.

4.8 DJX Co has entered into a contract to lease a vehicle for four years. Ownership of the vehicle will not be transferred at the end of the lease term and there are no options to either extend or terminate the lease.

Over what period should the vehicle be depreciated?

- ○ From the commencement of the lease to the end of the lease term
- ○ From the commencement of the lease to the end of the useful life of the vehicle ✓
- ☑ From the commencement of the lease to the earlier of the end of the lease term and the end of the useful life of the vehicle
- ○ From the commencement of the lease to the later of the end of the lease term and the end of the useful life of the vehicle

---

4.9 On 1 January 20X4 KLH Co took out a nine-month lease on a photocopier with payments of $1,440 per month, payable in arrears. As an incentive to enter into the lease, KLH Co received the first month rent free.

What amount in respect of this lease should be charged to profit or loss at KLH Co's year-end date of 31 March 20X4?

$ 3840 ✓

4.10 PVR Co enters into a contract to lease an asset on 1 July 20X6. It is required to pay four annual instalments of $3,000 in arrears. The present value of the lease payments not paid on 1 July 20X6 is $10,500 and the interest rate implicit in the lease is 7%.

What amount will be included in finance costs in respect of this lease in the statement of profit or loss for the year ended 30 June 20X9?

- ● $407
- ○ $576
- ○ $525 ✓
- ○ $351

4.11 On 1 April 20X5 ABR Co arranged to lease a building for four years at a rent of $50,000 per annum, paid in advance. There is an option to extend the lease for a further two years and ABR Co expects to exercise that option. The present value of lease payments not paid at 1 April 20X5 is $160,000 and the interest rate implicit in the lease is 9%.

What is the total amount charged to profit or loss in respect of this lease during the year to 31 March 20X6?

XT. 174400

$ 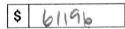 61196

50000 X

4.12 VWR Co obtained an asset under a lease on 1 May 20X3. It paid a deposit of $7,000 and incurred direct costs of $3,000. The present value of lease payments not paid at 1 May 20X3 was $85,000 and VWR Co received a lease incentive of $5,000.

What was the initial measurement of the right-of-use asset?

- ○ $90,000
- ○ $95,000
- ○ $92,000
- ○ $100,000

4.13 On 1 January 20X2 TKU Co hired a machine for a four-year period under a lease, with payments made in arrears. The machine had a five-year useful life. There is no option to extend the lease and no purchase option. The present value of lease payments not paid at 1 January 20X2 was $75,000 and the interest rate implicit in the lease was 8%. TKU Co incurred initial direct costs of $5,000.

What was the total amount charged to profit or loss in respect of this lease during the year to 31 December 20X2?

○ $26,400

○ $26,000

○ $25,150

○ $24,750

4.14 SBZ Co obtained an asset under a lease on 1 December 20X3. Payments of $14,000 per annum were to be paid in advance, commencing on 1 December 20X3, and the present value of lease payments not paid at the commencement date was $74,000. At the end of the lease period the asset will have to be decommissioned and the present value of the decommissioning cost at 1 December 20X3 was $12,000. *74OW.*

What was the initial measurement of the right-of-use asset?

$ | 100, 000   ✓

4.15 Which TWO of the following are amounts in respect of leases which lessees are required to disclose in accordance with IFRS 16 *Leases*?

○ Depreciation charge for the year in respect of right-of-use assets

○ Fair value of all right-of-use assets at the year end

○ Interest expense on lease liabilities

○ Total of lease incentives received

5 Other accounting standards

5.1 Which of the following would be an *internal* indicator of impairment of a machine, according to IAS 36 *Impairment of Assets*?

○ The market value of the machine has fallen significantly.

○ There have been significant changes in the technological environment affecting the business in which the machine is used.

Ⓞ/ The operating performance of the machine has declined.   ✓

○ The machine is fully depreciated.

5.2 The following values relate to a non-current asset: *RA*

FLL   lah

- Carrying amount $20,000
- Net realisable value $18,000
- Value in use $22,000
- Replacement cost $50,000

What is the recoverable amount of the asset?

- ○ $18,000
- ○ $20,000
- ◉ $22,000 ✓
- ○ $50,000

5.3 BI owns a building which it uses as its offices, warehouse and garage. The land is carried as a separate non-current tangible asset in the statement of financial position.

BI has a policy of regularly revaluing its non-current tangible assets. The original cost of the building in October 20X2 was $1,000,000; it was assumed to have a remaining useful life of 20 years at that date, with no residual value. The building was revalued on 30 September 20X4 by a professional valuer at $1,800,000.

The economic climate deteriorated during 20X5, causing BI to carry out an impairment review of its assets at 30 September 20X5. BI's building was valued at a market value of $1,500,000 on 30 September 20X5 by an independent valuer.

Calculate the impairment loss suffered at 30 September 20X5 and, using the picklist, select whether it should be recognised as part of BI's profit or loss for the period or in other comprehensive income.

$ [300,000]   [▼]

Handwritten: CA7 FVLC 1 800,000 · 1000,000 · ✗ · p.72

Picklist:
Recognise in profit or loss
Recognise in other comprehensive income

5.4 A machine has a carrying amount of $144,000. It could be sold for $133,200 with disposal costs of $3,600. Its current replacement cost is $250,000 and its value in use is estimated at $150,000. *129,600* · *150,000*

In accordance with IAS 36 *Impairment of Assets*, what (if any) is the impairment loss that should be recognised in respect of this machine?

- ○ $7,200
- ○ $6,000
- ○ $13,200 ✓
- ◉ $0

Handwritten: 21000 · (10500) · CA 10500 · 700

5.5 DS purchased a machine on 1 October 20X2 at a cost of $21,000. The machine had an expected useful life of six years with no expected residual value. DS depreciates its machines using the straight-line basis.

The machine has been used and depreciated for three years to 30 September 20X5. New technology was invented in December 20X5, before the financial statements for the year ended 30 September 20X5 were authorised for issue, which enabled a cheaper, more efficient machine to be produced. The board of DS have realised that this new technology will make their type of machine obsolete in the next couple of years and have concluded that their machine has a fair value of $9,200 and a value in use of $9,000. Disposal costs of $500 would be incurred were DS to sell the machine. *92w - 5w = 8700 ✗*

Calculate the impairment loss to be recognised in the financial statements for the year ended 30 September 20X5.

$ | 1800

5.6 Company X closed one of its divisions 12 months ago. It has yet to dispose of one remaining machine. The carrying amount of the machine at the date when business ceased was $750,000. It was being depreciated at 25% on a reducing balance basis. Company X has been advised that the fair value of the machine is $740,000 and expects to incur costs of $10,000 in making the sale. It has located a probable buyer but the sale will not be completed before the year end.

At what amount should the machine be shown in the year-end financial statements of Company X?

O $562,500

O $730,000

O $740,000

O $750,000

5.7 At its year end of 31 March 20X4 Macey has a machine on hand that it intends to sell in the next few months. It has identified several possible buyers and has priced the machine fairly according to the current market.

How should the machine be accounted for in the financial statements at 31 March 20X4 in accordance with IFRS 5 Non-current Assets Held for Sale and Discontinued Operations?

O   Continue to recognise the machine within property, plant and equipment but no longer depreciate it

O   Disclose the machine separately from other property, plant and equipment and no longer depreciate it

O   Continue to recognise the machine within property, plant and equipment and depreciate it

O   Disclose the machine separately from other property, plant and equipment but continue to depreciate it

---

5.8 BJ is an entity based in Europe that provides a range of facilities for holidaymakers and travellers.

At 1 October 20X4 these included:

• A short haul airline operating within Europe

• A travel agency specialising in arranging holidays to more exotic destinations, such as Hawaii and Fiji

BJ's airline operation has made significant losses for the last two years. On 31 January 20X5, the directors of BJ decided that, due to a significant increase in competition on short-haul flights within Europe, BJ would close all of its airline operations and dispose of its fleet of aircraft. All flights for holidaymakers and travellers who had already booked seats would be provided by third-party airlines. All operations ceased on 31 May 20X5.

On 31 July 20X5, BJ sold its fleet of aircraft and associated non-current assets for $500 million; the carrying amount at that date was $750 million.

At the reporting date, BJ was still in negotiation with some employees regarding severance payments. BJ has estimated that in the financial period October 20X5 to September 20X6, it will agree a settlement of $20 million compensation. The airline operation made a loss for the year ended 30 September 20X5 of $100 million.

The closure of the airline operation caused BJ to carry out a major restructuring of the entire entity. The restructuring has been agreed by the directors and active steps have been taken to implement it. The cost of restructuring to be incurred in the year 20X5/X6 is estimated at $10 million.

Calculate the loss that should be disclosed on the statement of profit or loss and other comprehensive income for the year ended 30 September 20X5, assuming that BJ makes the minimum disclosure required in relation to IFRS 5 *Non-current Assets Held for Sale and Discontinued Operations.*

$

5.9 On 1 March 20X5, the directors of YS decided to sell YS's manufacturing division. The division was available for immediate sale, but YS had not succeeded in disposing of the operation by 31 August 20X5 (the reporting date). YS identified a potential buyer for the division, but negotiations were ongoing; the directors are, however, certain that the sale will be completed within the next three months.

The manufacturing division's carrying amount at 1 March 20X5 was $443,000 and it had a fair value of $423,000.

YS's directors have estimated that YS will incur consultancy and legal fees for the disposal of $25,000.

Calculate the value of the impairment loss suffered by YS on classification of the manufacturing division as held for sale.

$

5.10 MN has a year end of 31 March and operates a number of retail outlets around the country. One retail outlet was closed on 31 March 20X1 when trading ceased and the outlet was put up for sale. The directors are certain that the outlet meets the requirements of IFRS 5 *Non-current Assets Held for Sale and Discontinued Operations* for treatment as non-current assets held for sale.

The carrying amounts of the property, plant and equipment held by the discontinued operation at the beginning of the year were as follows:

Asset type	Cost – discontinued operations $'000	Accumulated Depreciation – discontinued operations $'000	Carrying amount $'000
Land	150	0	150
Buildings	40	20	20
Plant and equipment	60	35	25
	250	55	195

MN depreciates buildings at 5% per annum on the straight-line basis and plant and equipment at 20% per annum using the reducing balance method.

The fair value less costs of disposal of the assets of the closed retail outlet at 31 March 20X1 was $176,000.

Calculate the impairment loss on the assets of the closed retail outlet on 31 March 20X1 when they were classified as held for sale.

$ [   ]

5.11 **Under IFRS 5, which TWO of the following are NOT factors in an operation being treated as a discontinued activity in the financial statements?**

☐ The sale or closure must be completed by the end of the reporting period.

☐ It represents a separate line of business.

☐ The anticipated sale is an associate acquired exclusively with a view to resale.

☐ The sale or closure is part of a single co-ordinated plan to dispose of a major line of business.

5.12 **Which FOUR of the following items SHOULD be included in arriving at the cost of the inventory of finished goods held by a manufacturing company, according to IAS 2 *Inventories*?**

☐ Carriage inwards on raw materials delivered to factory

☐ Carriage outwards on goods delivered to customers

☐ Factory supervisors' salaries

☐ Factory heating and lighting

☐ Cost of abnormally high idle time in the factory

☐ Import duties on raw materials

5.13 Shah's Shoes manufactures footwear. At the end of the year, 1,000 pairs of one line remain in inventory.

The costs involved in the manufacturing process are $3 in materials and $4 in labour per pair. The 1,000 pairs of shoes in inventory at the year end account for an estimated 2% of the factory's $100,000 annual overheads.

Selling costs are estimated at $2 per pair. The recommended retail price is $30 per pair, but Shah's normally sells them wholesale at 50% of this price. Sales have recently been flagging, compelling Shah's to offer a 30% trade discount on the wholesale price.

Calculate the value of inventory at the year end in accordance with IAS 2.

○ $8,500

○ $9,000

○ $10,500

○ $11,000

5.14 **Which THREE of the following describe situations where the net realisable value of inventory will be less than cost?**

☐ Increases in the selling price of goods sold

☐ Physical deterioration of inventory

☐ Increases in the cost of raw materials

☐ Errors in production or purchasing

5.15 An accountant is proposing to include overheads in closing inventory.

Which of the following statements correctly describes the treatment of overheads?

○ Overheads may be included provided the absorption rates reflect normal activity levels.

○ Overheads must not be included.

○ Only under-recoveries of overheads may be included.

○ The treatment is acceptable provided only production related overheads are included using a normal basis of activity to calculate the absorption rates.

5.16 **Which TWO of the following statements are correct?**

☐ Replacement cost is calculated as the selling price of the inventory less any further costs to completion or costs of selling the inventory.

☐ Average cost calculates a new weighted average cost upon each delivery.

☐ FIFO assumes that inventory is used in the order in which it is delivered.

☐ Inventory may not be valued using a standard cost.

☐ Net realisable value (NRV) values inventory at the current cost of acquisition.

5.17 DT's final dividend for the year ended 31 October 20X5 of $150,000 was declared on 1 February 20X6 and paid in cash on 1 April 20X6. The financial statements were approved on 31 March 20X6.

Which TWO of the following statements reflect the correct treatment of the dividend?

☐ The payment clears an accrued liability set up as at 31 October 20X5.

☐ The dividend is shown as a deduction in the statement of profit or loss and other comprehensive income for the year ended 31 October 20X6.

☐ The dividend is shown as an accrued liability as at 31 October 20X6.

☐ The $150,000 dividend was shown in the notes to the financial statements at 31 October 20X5.

☐ The dividend is shown as a deduction in the statement of changes in equity for the year ended 31 October 20X6.

5.18 **Which THREE of the following events after the reporting period would normally be classified as non-adjusting, according to IAS 10 *Events after the Reporting Period*?**

☐ Opening new trading operations

☐ Sale of goods held at the year end for less than cost

☐ A customer is discovered to be insolvent

☐ Announcement of plan to discontinue an operation

☐ Expropriation (seizure) of major assets by government

5.19 A company's statement of profit or loss and other comprehensive income showed a profit before tax of $1,800,000.

After the year end and before the financial statements were authorised for issue, the following events took place.

(1) The value of an investment held at the year end fell by $85,000.

(2) A customer who owed $116,000 at the year end went bankrupt.

(3) Inventory valued at cost of $161,000 in the statement of financial position was sold for $141,000.

(4) Assets with a carrying amount at the year end of $240,000 were unexpectedly seized by the local government.

What is the company's profit after making the necessary adjustments for these events?

○ $1,399,000

○ $1,579,000

○ $1,664,000

○ $1,800,000

5.20 GD's financial reporting period is 1 September 20X7 to 31 August 20X8.

Assuming that all amounts are material and that GD's financial statements have not yet been approved for publication, which one of the following would be classified as a non-adjusting event according to IAS 10 *Events after the Reporting Period*?

○ On 30 October 20X8, GD received a communication stating that one of its customers had ceased trading and gone into liquidation. The balance outstanding at 31 August 20X8 was unlikely to be paid.

○ At 31 August 20X8, GD had not provided for an outstanding legal action against the local government administration for losses suffered as a result of incorrect enforcement of local business regulations. On 5 November 20X8, the court awarded GD $50,000 damages.

○ On 1 October 20X8, GD made a rights issue of 1 new share for every 3 shares held at a price of $175. The market price on that date was $200.

○ At 31 August 20X8, GD had an outstanding insurance claim of $150,000. On 10 October 20X8, the insurance company informed GD that it would pay $140,000 as settlement.

6 Presentation of published financial statements

6.1 In accordance with IAS 1 *Presentation of Financial Statements*, which of the following MUST be disclosed on the face of the statement of profit or loss rather than by way of a note?

- ○ Other operating income
- ○ Depreciation
- ○ Finance costs ✓
- ○ Dividends paid

✓

6.2 The following information is an extract from DFG Co's trial balance for the year ended 31 March 20X7:

	Dr $	Cr $
5% loan notes (issued 20X5, redeemable 20X9)		280,000
Cash and cash equivalents		63,000
Cost of sales	554,000	
Distribution costs	140,000	
Inventory at 31 March 20X7	186,000	
Sales revenue		1,275,000
Trade payables		61,000
Trade receivables	175,000	

Additional information:

The sales revenue for the year to 31 March 20X7 includes $15,000 received from a new overseas customer. The $15,000 was a 10% deposit for an order of $150,000 worth of goods. DFG Co is still waiting for the results of the new customer's credit reference and at 31 March 20X7 had not despatched any goods.

Calculate the amounts for revenue and current assets that will be included in DFG Co's financial statements for the year ended 31 March 20X7.

	$	
Revenue	1260000	✓
Current assets	361,000	✓

6.3 Which of the following is true concerning the statement of changes in equity?

- ○ It reports all realised profits and losses only.
- ○ It does not include revaluation surpluses. ✗ ✓
- ○ It includes other comprehensive income. ✓
- ○ All of the above

6.4 The following information is an extract from Leapfrog Co's trial balance for the year ended 31 December 20X4:

	$	$
Administrative expenses	455,000	
Distribution costs	230,000	
Inventory purchases	1,425,000	
Inventory at 1 January 20X4	420,000	
Land and buildings at cost	2,500,000	
Plant and equipment – cost	1,055,000	
Building – accumulated depreciation at 1 January 20X4		225,000
Plant and equipment – accumulated depreciation at 1 January 20X4		400,000
Sales revenue		3,335,000
Trade receivables	330,000	

Additional information:

(a) Depreciation is charged on buildings using the straight-line method at a rate of 3% per annum and is recognised as an administrative expense. The cost of land included in land and buildings is $900,000.

(b) On 1 February 20X5, Leapfrog Co was informed that one of its customers, Piper Co, had ceased trading. The liquidators have advised Leapfrog Co that it is very unlikely to receive payment of any of the $36,000 due from Piper Co at 31 December 20X4. Irrecoverable debts are recognised within administrative expenses.

Calculate the amount that would be shown for revenue and administrative expenses in Leapfrog Co's statement of profit or loss for the year ended 31 December 20X4.

Revenue $ 3 335 000 ✓

Administrative expenses $ 539 000 ✗

6.5 BCW Co's statement of financial position shows capital and reserves figures for the years ended 31.12.X1 and 31.12.X2, as indicated in the table.

	20X2 $'000	20X1 $'000
Ordinary share capital	500	400
Share premium	20	0
Revaluation surplus	150	75
Retained earnings	400	340
	1,070	815

Dividends of $50,000 were paid during the year ended 31.12.X2.

What is BCW Co's total comprehensive income for the year as reported in the statement of profit and loss and other comprehensive income?

- ☑ $185,000
- ○ $135,000
- ○ $255,000
- ○ $110,000

6.6 The following information is an extract from DFG Co's trial balance for the year ended 31 March 20X7:

	Dr $	Cr $
Administrative expenses	180,000	
Cost of sales	554,000	
Distribution costs	140,000	
Inventory at 31 March 20X7	186,000	
Land and buildings at cost	960,000	
Plant and equipment at cost	480,000	
Buildings – accumulated depreciation at 1 April 20X6		33,000
Provision for plant and equipment depreciation at 1 April 20X6		234,000

Additional information:

(a) There were no sales of non-current assets during the year ended 31 March 20X7.

(b) Depreciation is charged on buildings using the straight-line method at 3% per annum. The cost of land included in land and buildings is $260,000. Buildings depreciation is treated as an administrative expense.

(c) Up to 31 March 20X6 all plant and equipment was depreciated using the straight-line method at 12.5%. However, some plant and equipment has been wearing out and needing to be replaced on average after six years. DFG Co's management has therefore decided that from 1 April 20X6 the expected useful life of this type of plant and equipment should be changed to a total of six years from acquisition. The plant and equipment affected was purchased on 1 April 20X2 and had an original cost of $120,000. This plant and equipment is estimated to have no residual value. All plant and equipment depreciation should be charged to cost of sales.

Calculate the amount for cost of sales that will be included in DFG Co's statement of profit or loss and other comprehensive income for the year ended 31 March 20X7.

	$
Cost of sales	

6.7   Burrows Co is a soft drinks manufacturer.

Which of the following items must be disclosed on the face of the statement of profit or loss?

All items are material.

- ☑ Loss on closure of bottling division
- ○ Irrecoverable debt as a result of bankruptcy of a major customer
- ○ Profit on a sale of outdated mixing machinery
- ○ Fall in value of head office building due to recession   ✓

6.8   On 31 December 20X4, Leapfrog Co sold some obsolete plant and equipment for $3,000. The plant and equipment had originally cost $46,000 and had a carrying amount of $5,000. The purchaser has not yet paid for the plant and equipment and Leapfrog Co has not made any entries in its financial records for this disposal.

Show the journal entry Leapfrog Co should make to record the disposal of the obsolete plant and equipment in their accounting records.

	Dr $	Cr $
P+E cost	~~2000~~	46000
P+E acc	41000	
loss on dis	2000	
Recieve	3000	~~4000~~

Picklist:

Buildings – accumulated depreciation
Cash and cash equivalents
Loss on disposal of non-current assets   ✓
Payables
Plant and equipment – accumulated depreciation
Plant and equipment – cost
Profit on disposal of non-current assets
Receivables

6.9   **Which of the following might appear as a separate item in the other comprehensive income section of the statement of profit or loss and other comprehensive income?**

- ○ A material irrecoverable debt arising in the year
- ○ A share issue in the year
- ○ An impairment loss on assets carried at depreciated historical cost   ∨
- ☑ An upward revaluation of the company's assets

6.10   The following information is an extract from DFG Co's trial balance for the year ended
        31 March 20X7:

	Dr $	Cr $
5% $1 loan notes (issued 20X5, redeemable 20X9)		280,000
Administrative expenses	180,000	
Cost of sales	554,000	
Distribution costs	140,000	
Inventory at 31 March 20X7	186,000	
Land and buildings at cost	960,000	
Loan interest paid	7,000	
Plant and equipment at cost	480,000	
Buildings – accumulated depreciation at 1 April 20X6		33,000
Plant and equipment – accumulated depreciation at 1 April 20X6		234,000

Additional information:

(a)   There were no sales of non-current assets during the year ended 31 March 20X7.

(b)   Depreciation is charged on buildings using the straight-line method at 3% per
        annum. The cost of land included in land and buildings is $260,000. Buildings
        depreciation is treated as an administrative expense.

(c)   Up to 31 March 20X6 all plant and equipment was depreciated using the straight-line
        method at 12.5%. However, some plant and equipment has been wearing out and
        needing to be replaced on average after six years. DFG Co's management has
        therefore decided that from 1 April 20X6 the expected useful life of this type of plant
        and equipment should be changed to a total of six years from acquisition. The plant
        and equipment affected was purchased on 1 April 20X2 and had an original cost of
        $120,000. This plant and equipment is estimated to have no residual value. All plant
        and equipment depreciation should be charged to cost of sales.

Calculate the amounts for administrative expenses and finance costs that will be
included in DFG Co's statement of profit or loss and other comprehensive income for
the year ended 31 March 20X7.

	$
Administrative expenses	201 000
Finance costs	7 000

14000 loan

7 paid DW

6.11　B Co had the following transactions in non-current assets during the year to 31 October 20X9:

- A $16,000 write down in the value of some items of plant held at historical cost
- Upward revaluation of offices by $92,000

What is the total amount that will be reported in other comprehensive income by B Co in relation to these transactions?

○　$(16,000) loss

◎　$92,000 gain

○　$76,000 gain

○　$(16,000) loss and $92,000 gain separately disclosed

6.12　The following information is an extract from Leapfrog Co's trial balance for the year ended 31 December 20X4:

	$	$
Inventory purchases	1,425,000	
Inventory at 1 January 20X4	420,000	
Plant and equipment – cost	1,055,000	
Plant and equipment – accumulated depreciation at 1 January 20X4		400,000

Additional information:

(a)　On 31 December 20X4, Leapfrog Co sold obsolete plant and equipment which had a carrying amount of $5,000 and this transaction resulted in a loss on disposal of $2,000. The transaction has not yet been accounted for but any gain or loss on disposal should be included in cost of sales.

(b)　Closing inventory at 31 December 20X4 was $562,000.

(c)　Plant and equipment is depreciated using the reducing balance method at a rate of 30%. Depreciation of, and any gains or losses relating to, the disposal of plant and equipment are recognised within cost of sales.

What is the figure for cost of sales that should be shown in Leapfrog Co's statement of profit or loss for the year ended 31 December 20X4?

○　$1,478,000

○　$1,479,500

◎　$1,480,000

·○　$1,481,500

6.13　D Co's transactions and results for the period to 31 December 20X9 are shown in the table:

	$m
Profit for the period	29
Surplus on property 1 revaluation	14
Deficit on property 2 revaluation	(7)
Issue of share capital	1

Property 1 had previously been revalued upwards by $8 million. Property 2 had previously been revalued upwards by $10 million.

What amount would appear in the statement of changes in equity as total comprehensive income for the period?

- ○ $30 million
- ○ $36 million
- ○ $37 million
- ○ $43 million

6.14   The following information is an extract from DFG Co's trial balance for the year ended 31 March 20X7:

	Dr $	Cr $
5% $1 loan notes (issued 20X5, redeemable 20X9)		280,000
Equity dividend paid 1 September 20X6	55,000	
Income tax	10,000	
Loan interest paid	7,000	
Ordinary shares $1 each, fully paid at 1 April 20X6		560,000
Retained earnings at 1 April 20X6		121,000
Share premium		120,000
Trade payables		61,000

Additional information:

(a)   The income tax balance in the trial balance is a result of the under-provision of tax for the year ended 31 March 20X6.

(b)   The tax due for the year ended 31 March 20X7 is estimated at $52,000.

Calculate the amounts for the tax expense, current tax payable, share capital and share premium that will be included in DFG Co's financial statements for the year ended 31 March 20X7.

	$
Tax expense	62,000
Current tax payable	52,000
Share capital	560,000
Share premium	120,000

6.15   The following information is an extract from Leapfrog Co's trial balance for the year ended
        31 December 20X4:

	$	$
Equity dividend paid	360,000	
Equity shares $1 each, fully paid at 31 December 20X4		1,500,000
Retained earnings at 1 January 20X4		370,000
Share premium at 31 December 20X4		250,000

Additional information:

(a)   On 1 July 20X4, Leapfrog Co issued 50,000 new equity shares at a premium of 20%.
       All proceeds from the share issue were received and have been included in the trial
       balance.

(b)   During the year Leapfrog Co also paid a final dividend of $240,000 in respect of the
       year ended 31 December 20X3 and an interim dividend on 31 July 20X4 for the year
       ended 31 December 20X4.

**Complete the entries that would be shown in the shaded boxes in Leapfrog Co's
statement of changes in equity for the year ended 31 December 20X4.**

	Share capital $'000	Share premium $'000	Retained earnings $'000	Total $'000
Balance at 1 January 20X4	1,500,000	240,000	370,000	
Share issue	50,000	100,000		
Dividend paid			360,000	
Profit for the period			10,000	
Balance at 31 December 20X4	1,500,000	250,000	X	X

---

7   Statements of cash flows

7.1   In a statement of cash flows which of the following would NOT be shown as a cash
       flow within the cash flows from financing section?

       ○   Issue of ordinary shares

       ○   Repurchase of a long-term loan

       ○   Dividends paid

       ⊘   Repayment of an overdraft

7.2   Which one of the items below would NOT appear in the statement of cash flows?

       ○   Cash receipts from customers

       ○   A dividend paid to preference shareholders in the year

       ○   Repayment of a bank loan

       ○   The statement of profit or loss charge for taxation for the current year

---

7.3 In a company's statement of cash flows, a revaluation of non-current assets during the year will be:

○ Shown as an adjustment to profit before tax

○ Shown as a cash inflow

○ Disclosed under investing activities

○ Entirely excluded

7.4 In a statement of cash flows, which of the items below would NOT appear as a cash outflow?

○ The nominal value of loan notes redeemed at par during the year

○ The dividends paid to preference shareholders during the year

○ The statement of profit or loss charge for depreciation for the year

○ The purchase of long-term investments

7.5 The following balances appear in the statement of financial position of Peterson Co.

	Year ending 31 October	
	20X4	*20X3*
	$'000	$'000
Share capital	1,600	1,200
Share premium	400	280

What figure would appear in the statement of cash flows for the proceeds from the issue of shares? Give your answer to the nearest $'000.

$'000	

7.6 The following balances appear in the statement of financial position of Lea Co.

	Year ending 31 March	
	20X5	*20X4*
	$	$
Non-current assets at cost	1,250,000	1,096,000
Revaluation surplus	240,000	140,000

During the year ended 31 March 20X5 non-current assets with a cost of $150,000 were disposed of.

Calculate the amount that would appear in the statement of cash flows for the purchase of non-current assets.

$	

7.7 Carrie Co is preparing its statement of cash flows.

Which of the following would need to be deducted from profit before tax in order to generate a figure for cash flows from operating activities?

○ Write down for irrecoverable debts

○ Write down for obsolete inventory

○ Surplus on revaluation of property

○ Gain on sale of a motor vehicle

7.8 The statement of cash flows is based on 'cash and cash equivalents' as defined by IAS 7 *Statement of Cash Flows*.

Which FOUR of the following items could be included in cash?

☑ Bank current account in domestic currency

☐ Short-term deposit (three-month notice period)

☐ Bank overdraft

☐ Petty cash float

☐ Bank current account in foreign currency

7.9 Information concerning the non-current assets of Ealing Co is detailed in the table below.

During the year non-current assets which had cost $80,000 and which had a carrying amount of $30,000 were sold for $20,000.

The final figure for net cash flows from operating activities for the year was $300,000.

	Start of year $	End of year $
Cost	180,000	240,000
Accumulated depreciation	(120,000)	(140,000)
Carrying amount	60,000	100,000

Non-current assets were not revalued during the year.

What was the increase in cash and cash equivalents for the year?

○ $240,000

○ $260,000

○ $180,000

○ $320,000

7.10 At 1 October 20X4, BK had a balance of accrued interest payable amounting to $12,000.

During the year ended 30 September 20X5, BK charged interest payable of $41,000 to its statement of profit of loss and other comprehensive income.

The closing balance on accrued interest payable account at 30 September 20X5 was $15,000.

BPP
LEARNING
MEDIA

How much interest paid should BK show on its statement of cash flows for the year ended 30 September 20X5?

- ⊘ $38,000
- ○ $41,000
- ○ $44,000
- ○ $53,000

7.11 A statement of cash flows shows the increase or decrease in cash and cash equivalents in the period.

Which THREE of the following items are included in this movement?

- ☑ Cash at a bank
- ☑ Bank overdraft
- ☑ Current asset investments readily convertible into known amounts of cash and which can be sold without disrupting the company's business
- ☐ Equity investments
- ☐ Long-term loans

7.12 **Which THREE of the following items should NOT appear in a company's statement of cash flows?**

- ☑ Proposed dividends
- ☐ Dividends received
- ☑ Bonus issue of shares
- ☑ Surplus on revaluation of a non-current asset
- ☐ Proceeds of sale of an investment not connected with the company's trading activities

---

7.13 **Which one of the following would need to be deducted from profit before tax in order to generate a figure for net cash from operating activities?**

- ○ Amortisation charge for the year
- ○ Surplus on revaluation of property
- ○ Capital element of a loan repayment
- ○ Profit on sale of a non-current asset

7.14 Blacksmith disposes of an asset with a carrying amount of $21,000 for $30,000 on 7 July 20X1.

How will this transaction be disclosed in the statement of cash flows?

- ○ Cash flows from operating activities reconciliation: $(9,000); Cash inflow: $30,000
- ○ Cash flows from operating activities reconciliation: $9,000; Cash inflow: $30,000
- ○ Cash flows from operating activities reconciliation: $(21,000); Cash inflow: $30,000
- ○ Cash flows from operating activities reconciliation: $21,000; Cash inflow: $30,000

7.15 RTS Co has leased a vehicle over a four-year term. Capital amounts repaid under the lease during the year to 31 December 20X3 amounted to $17,000.

How will this amount be shown in the statement of cash flows?

○ It will be deducted in arriving at cash flows from operating activities.

○ It will be added back in arriving at cash flows from operating activities.

○ It will be shown as a cash outflow under investing activities. ✓

◔ It will be shown as a cash outflow under financing activities.

8 General principles of taxation

8.1 **Which of the following statements is correct?**

○ Tax evasion is legally arranging affairs so as to minimise the tax liability. Tax avoidance is the illegal manipulation of the tax system to avoid paying taxes due.

○ Tax evasion is legally arranging affairs so as to evade paying tax. Tax avoidance is tax planning – legally arranging affairs so as to minimise the tax liability.

○ Tax evasion is using loopholes in legislation to evade paying tax. Tax avoidance is the illegal manipulation of the tax system to avoid paying taxes due.

○ Tax evasion is the illegal manipulation of the tax system to avoid paying taxes due. Tax avoidance is tax planning – legally arranging affairs so as to minimise the tax liability.

8.2 **Which ONE of the following defines the meaning of 'tax gap'?**

○ The difference between the tax an entity expects to pay and the amount notified by the tax authority

○ The difference between the total amount of tax due to be paid and the amount actually collected by the tax authority

○ The difference between the due date for tax payment and the date it is actually paid

○ The difference between the amount of tax provided in the financial statements and the amount actually paid

8.3 An ideal tax system should conform to certain principles.

Which one of the following statements is NOT generally regarded as a principle of an ideal tax?

○ It should be fair to different individuals and should reflect a person's ability to pay.

○ It should not be arbitrary, it should be certain.

○ It should raise as much money as possible for the government.

○ It should be convenient in terms of timing and payment.

8.4 Which one of the following powers is a tax authority LEAST likely to have granted to them?

- ○ Power of arrest
- ○ Power to examine records
- ○ Power of entry and search
- ○ Power to give information to another country's tax authorities

8.5 Which of the following is LEAST likely to be a reason for governments to set deadlines for filing returns and paying taxes?

- ○ To help taxpayers know when to pay their taxes
- ○ To enable the tax authority to forecast its cash flow more accurately
- ○ To provide a reference point for penalties for late payment
- ○ To ensure tax is paid early

8.6 What is 'hypothecation'?

- ○ The process of earmarking tax revenues for specific types of expenditure
- ○ An estimation of tax revenue made by the tax authorities for budget purposes
- ○ A refund made by tax authorities for tax paid in other countries
- ○ The payment of taxes due to tax authorities, net of tax refunds due from tax authorities

8.7 An entity sells furniture and adds a sales tax to the selling price of all products sold. A customer purchasing furniture from the entity has to pay the cost of the furniture plus the sales tax. The customer therefore bears the cost of the sales tax.

What type of incidence is this referred to as?

- ○ Formal incidence
- ○ Indirect incidence
- ○ Effective incidence
- ○ Direct incidence

8.8 The term 'tax gap' describes the difference between:

- ○ When a tax payment is due and the date it is actually paid
- ○ The tax due calculated by the entity and the tax demanded by the tax authority
- ○ The amount of tax due to be paid and the amount actually collected
- ○ The date when the entity was notified by the tax authority of the tax due and the date on which the tax should be paid

8.9   BM has a taxable profit of $30,000 and receives a tax assessment of $3,000. BV has a taxable profit of $60,000 and receives a tax assessment of $7,500.

BM and BV are resident in the same tax jurisdiction.

Which tax rate structure operates in this jurisdiction?

- ○   A progressive tax
- ○   A regressive task
- ○   A direct tax
- ○   A proportional tax

8.10   **Which TWO of the following are MOST LIKELY to encourage an increase in the incidence of tax avoidance or tax evasion?**

- ☐   High penalties for any tax evasion
- ☐   Imprecise and vague tax laws
- ☐   A tax system that is seen as fair to everyone
- ☐   Very high tax rates

8.11   B buys goods from a wholesaler, paying the price of the goods plus sales tax (VAT). B sells goods in its shop to customers. The customers pay the price of the goods plus sales tax (VAT).

From the perspective of B, the sales tax (VAT) would have:

- ○   Effective incidence
- ○   Formal incidence
- ○   Ineffective incidence
- ○   Informal incidence

8.12   **Which of the following BEST describes the effective incidence of a tax?**

- ○   The date the tax is actually paid
- ○   The person or entity that finally bears the cost of the tax
- ○   The date the tax assessment is issued
- ○   The person or entity receiving the tax assessment

8.13   **Which ONE of the following powers is not available to tax authorities?**

- ○   Power to review and query filed returns
- ○   Power to detain company officials
- ○   Power to request special returns
- ○   Power to enter and search premises

8.14 Which of the following is the best definition of 'competent jurisdiction' for an entity paying tax?

- ○ The tax authority that knows the most about the type of taxes the entity pays
- ○ The tax authority whose tax laws apply to an entity
- ◉ The tax authority in the country where the entity has most of its operations
- ○ The tax authority which gives the entity the most accurate calculation of taxes payable

8.15 Select the relevant box to denote which tax term is being described.

	Tax avoidance	Tax evasion	Tax gap
The use of legitimate tax rules to minimise the amount of tax payable			
The difference between the tax theoretically collectable and the amount actually collected			
Seeking to pay too little tax by deliberately misleading the tax authorities		✓	

9 Direct taxation

9.1 RS purchased an asset on 1 April 20X0 for $375,000, incurring legal fees of $12,000. RS is resident in Country X. There was no indexation allowed on the asset.

RS sold the asset on 31 March 20X3 for $450,000, incurring transaction charges of $15,000.

Relevant tax rules

Corporate profits

The rules for taxation of corporate profits are as follows:

- The corporate tax on profits and capital gains is at a rate of 25%.

Calculate the capital gains tax due from RS on disposal of the asset. Give your answer to the nearest $.

$ | 12,000 |

9.2 Which one of the following is NOT a benefit of the pay-as-you-earn (PAYE) method of tax collection?

- ○ It makes payment of tax easier for the taxpayer as it is in instalments.
- ○ It makes it easier for governments to forecast tax revenues.
- ◉ It benefits the taxpayer as it reduces the tax payable.
- ○ It improves governments 'cash flow' as cash is received earlier.

BPP LEARNING MEDIA

9.3 **Which TWO of the following taxes would normally be defined as direct taxation?**

☐ Import duty payable on specific types of imported goods

☑ Individual income tax, usually deducted at source

☑ Corporate income tax

☐ Sales tax

9.4 An entity purchases new computer equipment for $72,000 during the year. The profit for the year (excluding depreciation) was $128,000.

The corporate income tax rate applicable to profits was 25%. The computer equipment qualified for first-year tax writing-down allowance of 50%.

Calculate the tax payable for the year. Give your answer to the nearest $.

$ 23,000

9.5 An entity, resident in Country X, had accumulated tax losses of $320,000 at 31 December 20X2. The entity had a taxable profit of $480,000 for the year ended 31 December 20X3.

Relevant tax rules

Corporate profits

The rules for taxation of corporate profits/losses in country X are as follows:

- Accounting rules on recognition and measurement are followed for tax purposes
- The corporate tax on profits is at a rate of 25%

Tax losses can be carried forward to offset against future taxable profits from the same business.

For the year ended 31 December 20X3 the entity will:

○ Pay no tax for the year and carry forward a loss of $200,000

○ Pay $10,000 tax for the year and have no loss to carry forward

◉ Pay $40,000 tax for the year and have no loss to carry forward

○ Pay $160,000 tax for the year and have no loss to carry forward

---

9.6 A Co has been trading for a number of years and is resident for tax purposes in Country X.

The tax written down value of A Co's property, plant and equipment was $40,000 at 31 March 20X8. A Co did not purchase any property, plant and equipment between 1 April 20X8 and 31 March 20X9.

A Co's statement of profit or loss for the year ended 31 March 20X9 is as follows:

	$
Gross profit	270,000
Administrative expenses	(120,000)
Depreciation – property, plant and equipment	(12,000)
Distribution costs	(55,000)
Finance cost	(11,000)
Profit before tax	72,000

Administration expenses include entertaining of $15,000.

Relevant tax rules

Corporate profits

The rules for taxation of corporate profits in country X are as follows:

- Accounting rules of recognition and measurement are followed for tax purposes.
- All expenses other than depreciation, amortisation, entertaining, taxes paid to other public bodies and donations to political parties are tax deductible.
- The corporate tax on profits is at a rate of 25%.

What is A Co's income tax due for the year ended 31 March 20X9?

- ○ $8,750
- ○ $13,750
- ○ $15,500
- ○ $22,250

9.7 **Which ONE of the following is regarded as a direct tax?**

- ○ Sales tax
- ○ Capital gains tax
- ○ Excise duties
- ○ Property tax

9.8 **Which ONE of the following gives the meaning of rollover relief?**

- ○ Trading losses can be carried forward to future years.
- ○ Inventory can be valued using current values instead of original cost.
- ○ Capital losses made in a period can be carried forward to future years.
- ○ Payment of tax on a capital gain can be delayed if the full proceeds from the sale of an asset are reinvested in a replacement asset.

BPP LEARNING MEDIA

9.9 P Co paid a dividend of $150,000 to its shareholders in the year ended 30 June 20X1. P Co is resident for tax purposes in Country X where the corporate rate of income tax is 25% and the personal rate of income tax is 30% on dividends received. Country X has an imputation system of tax.

How much tax is payable on the dividend received by the shareholders of P Co?

$ [ ]

9.10 An entity makes a taxable profit of $600,000 and pays corporate income tax at 25%. The entity pays a dividend to its shareholders. A shareholder who pays personal tax at 40% receives a $6,000 dividend then pays an additional $2,400 tax on the dividend.

The tax system could be said to be:

- ☑ A classical system
- ◯ An imputation system
- ◯ A split rate system
- ◯ A partial imputation system

9.11 An entity, resident in Country X, reported accounting profits of $500,000 for the period ended 30 September 20X4. The profit was after deducting entertaining expenses of $51,000 and a donation to a political party of $36,000.

The entity also included a non-taxable government grant receipt of $100,000 in its reported profit.

Relevant tax rules

Corporate profits

The rules for taxation of corporate profits in Country X are as follows:

- Accounting rules on recognition and measurement are followed for tax purposes.
- All expenses other than depreciation, amortisation, entertaining, taxes paid to other public bodies and donations to political parties are tax deductible.
- The corporate tax on profits is at a rate of 25%.

Calculate the entity's tax payable for the year ended 30 September 20X4. Give your answer to the nearest $.

$ [ ]

9.12 In Country X a company that is a member of a group can transfer its trading loss to another group member to offset against its taxable profits. This is called group relief.

Which TWO of the below are likely to be advantages of group relief?

- ☐ It enables tax to be saved at the highest marginal rate.
- ☐ It enables tax to be saved at the highest average rate.
- ☐ It improves the cash flow of the group by enabling the trading loss to be used as soon as possible.
- ☐ It enables more trading loss to be carried forward.

9.13 EH is resident in Country X. EH purchased an asset on 1 April 20X2 for $420,000, incurring additional import duties of $30,000. The relevant index increased by 40% in the period from 1 April 20X2 to 31 March 20X9.

EH sold the asset on 31 March 20X9 for $700,000, incurring selling costs of $10,000.

Relevant tax rules

Corporate profits

The rules for taxation of corporate profits in Country X are as follows:

- All purchase and selling costs are allowable for tax purposes.
- The corporate tax on profits and capital gains is at a rate of 25%.

How much tax was due from EH on disposal of its asset?

$ ☐

9.14 WYK Co is resident for tax purposes in Country X. The directors purchased an asset, which was eligible for tax depreciation, on 1 January 20X0 for $6,000. The asset is sold for $3,100 on 31 December 20X2.

Relevant tax rules

Corporate profits

The rules for taxation of corporate profits in Country X are as follows:

- Tax depreciation allowances are available on eligible assets at a rate of 50% in the year of acquisition and 25% on a reducing balance basis in subsequent years.

- There is no tax depreciation allowance in the year of disposal when a balancing charge or allowance will arise.

Complete the following sentence to show the amount of any balancing charge or balancing allowance. You should select the correct option from the picklist and enter the correct figure.

For the year ended 31 December 20X2 there is a balancing ☐▼ of

$ ☐ .

Picklist:

allowance
charge

9.15 SHM Co has a profit before tax of $300,000 for the year. This includes non-taxable income of $50,000 and depreciation relating to non-current assets of $30,000. In addition, expenses of $25,000 are disallowable for tax purposes and tax depreciation has been calculated as $24,000.

What is the taxable profit?

- ○ $279,000
- ○ $281,000
- ○ $319,000
- ○ $321,000

10 International and indirect taxation

10.1 Which of the following sentences best describes a withholding tax?

○ Tax withheld from payment to the tax authorities

○ Tax paid less an amount withheld from payment

○ Tax deducted at source before payment of interest or dividends

○ Tax paid on increases in value of investment holdings

10.2 Which of the following best describes the purpose of double tax relief?

○ To ensure that a company does not pay tax twice on any of its income

○ To mitigate taxing overseas income twice

○ To avoid taxing dividends received from subsidiaries in the same country twice

○ To provide relief where a company pays tax at double the normal rate

10.3 A country has a duty that is levied on all imported petroleum products. This levy is $5 per litre.

This duty could be said to be:

○ General consumption tax

○ Sales tax

○ Specific unit tax

○ Ad valorem tax

10.4 An entity sells household items such as kettles and toasters and adds sales tax to the selling price of all products sold. A customer purchasing the goods has to pay the cost of the goods plus sales tax. The entity pays the sales tax to the tax authority.

Which TWO of the following are appropriate classifications for the sales tax from the perspective of the entity?

☐ Direct tax

☐ Indirect tax

☐ Effective incidence

☐ Formal incidence

☐ Trading tax

10.5   HY is registered for sales tax in Country X.

HY purchased a consignment of goods for $70,000 plus sales tax at the standard rate and then sold the goods for $138,000 inclusive of sales tax at the standard rate.

Relevant tax rules

Sales tax

Country X has a sales tax system which allows entities to reclaim input tax paid.

The Country X sales tax rates are:

- Zero rated: 0%
- Standard rated: 15%
- Exempt goods: 0%

How much profit should HY record in its statement of profit or loss and other comprehensive income for this consignment?

○ $50,000

○ $57,500

○ $68,000

○ $77,130

10.6   **Which ONE of the following would be considered to be an example of an indirect tax?**

○   An entity assessed for corporate income tax on its profit

○   An individual who purchases goods in a shop – the price includes sales tax

○   An employee who has tax deducted from their salary through the PAYE system

○   An individual who pays capital gains tax on a gain arising on the disposal of an investment

---

10.7   **Which of the following is an indirect tax?**

○   Withholding tax

○   Employee tax

○   Sales tax

○   Corporate income tax

10.8   **Which of the following 'persons' bears the cost of a sales tax?**

○   The supplier of raw materials

○   The end consumer

○   The retailer

○   The wholesaler

10.9 When an entity is resident for tax purposes in more than one country, the OECD Model Tax Convention states that an entity will be deemed to be resident only in its:

○ Place of permanent establishment

○ Place of effective management

○ Place of incorporation

○ Place of main business activity

10.10 Tuton, a company resident in Country X, is a 100% owned subsidiary of Carmoon, a company resident in Country Y. At the year end, Tuton paid a dividend of $90,000 after deduction of withholding tax of $10,000, to Carmoon. Country Y charges corporate income tax at a rate of 40% and gives double tax relief by the credit method.

Below is an extract from Tuton's statement of profit or loss for the year.

	$'000
Gross profit	1,850
Tax	(240)
Net profit for the year	1,200

Underlying tax is $20,000.

How much double tax relief is given to Carmoon in Country Y?

$ [   ]

10.11 Where a resident entity runs an overseas operation as a branch of the entity, certain tax implications arise.

Which ONE of the following does NOT usually apply in relation to an overseas branch?

○ Assets can be transferred to the branch without triggering a capital gain.

○ Corporate income tax is paid on profits remitted by the branch.

○ Tax depreciation can be claimed on any qualifying assets used in the trade of the branch.

○ Losses sustained by the branch are immediately deductible against the resident entity's income.

10.12 HN purchases products from a foreign country. The products cost $14 each and are subject to excise duty of $3 per item and sales tax at the standard rate.

Sales tax is calculated on cost including the excise duty.

HN is resident in Country X.

Relevant tax rules

Sales tax

Country X has a sales tax system which allows entities to reclaim input tax paid.

The Country X sales tax rates are:

- Zero rated: 0%
- Standard rated: 15%
- Exempt goods: 0%

If HN imports 1,000 items, how much does it pay to the tax authorities for this transaction?

- ○ $2,100
- ○ $5,100
- ○ $5,550
- ○ $19,550

10.13 Ying, a company resident in Country A, is a 100% owned subsidiary of Yang, a company resident in Country B. At the year end, Ying paid a dividend of $80,000 to Yang, from which withholding tax of $12,000 was deducted. Country B charges corporate income tax at a rate of 30% and gives double tax relief by the credit method.

Below is an extract from Ying's statement of profit or loss for the year.

	$'000
Gross profit	2,130
Tax	(450)
Net profit for the year	900

Underlying tax is $40,000.

How much tax is payable by Yang in country B in respect of the dividend received from Ying?

$ [   ]

10.14 Company P has input tax for the quarter of $57,000. 50% of this is attributable to exempt outputs and the other 50% is attributable to zero-rated outputs.

How much input tax can it reclaim?

$ [   ]

10.15   A company has made sales in a period of $264,500, including sales tax. Its purchases excluding sales tax were $170,000, including zero-rated items of $20,000.

If the rate of sales tax is 15%, how much is payable to the tax authorities?

○ $12,000

○ $14,935

○ $17,175

○ $20,110

11   Working capital and the operating cycle

11.1   An entity's working capital financing policy is to finance working capital using short-term financing to fund all the fluctuating current assets as well as some of the permanent part of the current assets.

The above policy is an example of:

○   An aggressive policy

○   A conservative policy

○   A short-term policy

○   A moderate policy

11.2   Which of the following is NOT a symptom of overtrading?

○   Increasing levels of inventory

○   Increasing levels of trade receivables

○   Increasing levels of current liabilities

○   Increasing levels of long-term borrowings

11.3   The following information relates to Company X:

Trade receivables collection period	54 days
Raw material inventory turnover period	46 days
Work-in-progress inventory turnover period	32 days
Trade payables payment period	67 days
Finished goods inventory turnover period	43 days

What is the length of the working capital cycle?

○   134 days

○   156 days

⊘   108 days

○   150 days

11.4 Which of the following would NOT be associated with a company that is overtrading?

- ○ A dramatic reduction in sales revenue
- ○ A rapid increase in the outstanding overdraft amount
- ○ A rapid increase in the volume of inventory
- ○ A dramatic reduction in trade payables days

11.5 Which THREE of the following statements are true with regards to over capitalisation?

- ☐ Shareholders will not be happy as resources could be used elsewhere to generate a return.
- ☐ The entity has invested too much in non-current assets.
- ☐ The entity has invested too much in receivables, inventory and cash and holds few payables.
- ☐ The entity has an excess of working capital.
- ☐ The entity has invested too much in subsidiaries.

11.6 HMP has decided to adopt a moderate working capital policy. It has fluctuating current assets of $1 million, permanent current assets of $5 million, and non-current assets of $9 million.

Which of the following mixes of finance is the company MOST LIKELY to choose?

- ○ Short-term financing of $1 million; permanent financing of $14 million
- ○ Short-term financing of $0.5 million; permanent financing of $14.5 million
- ○ Short-term financing of $2 million; permanent financing of $13 million
- ○ Short-term financing of $4 million; permanent financing of $11 million

11.7 A company has annual sales revenues of $48 million. The company earns a constant gross margin of 40% on sales. All sales and purchases are on credit and are evenly distributed over the year.

The following are maintained at a constant level throughout the year:

Inventory	$8 million
Trade receivables	$10 million
Trade payables	$5 million

What is the company's cash operating cycle to the nearest day?

- ○ 99 days
- ○ 114 days
- ○ 89 days
- ○ 73 days

11.8 A company has annual sales revenues of $30 million and the following working capital periods:

Inventory conversion period   2.5 months

Accounts receivable collection period   2.0 months

Accounts payable equates to $2.625 million.

Production costs represent 70% of sales revenue.

Calculate the total amount held in working capital excluding cash and cash equivalents.

$ [   ] million

11.9 The following information has been calculated for a business:

Trade receivable collection period   54 days

Trade payables payments period   67 days

If the working capital cycle is 102 days, what is the inventory turnover period?

○   19 days

○   115 days

○   89 days

○   13 days

11.10 An extract from a company's trial balance at the end of its financial year is given below.

	$'000
Sales revenue (85% on credit)	2,600
Cost of sales	1,800
Purchases (90% on credit)	1,650
Inventory of finished goods	220
Trade receivables	350
Trade payables	260

Calculate the following working capital ratios. Give your answer to one decimal point.

Inventory days   [   ]

Trade receivables days   [   ]

11.11 **A company's working capital cycle can be calculated as:**

- ☑ Inventory days plus accounts receivable days less accounts payable days
- ○ Accounts receivable days plus accounts payable days less inventory days
- ○ Inventory days plus accounts payable days less accounts receivable days
- ○ Accounts payable days plus accounts receivable days plus inventory days

---

11.12 RS reviews the financial performance of potential customers before setting a credit limit. The summarised financial statements for PQ, a potential major customer operating in the retail industry, are shown below.

Summary statement of financial position for PQ at year end

	20X1	20X0
	$'000	$'000
Non-current assets	6,400	5,600
Inventories	1,200	1,120
Trade receivables	800	840
Cash	200	40
Trade payables	(1,120)	(1,160)
Non-current liabilities	(3,600)	(3,200)
Net assets	3,880	3,240
Share capital	2,400	2,400
Retained earnings	1,480	840
	3,880	3,240

Summary statement of profit or loss for PQ for the years

	20X1	20X0
	$'000	$'000
Sales	12,000	10,000
Cost of sales	6,400	5,200
Profit before interest and tax	2,400	1,800

Calculate the following ratios using average balances for PQ for 20X1. Give your answer to one decimal place.

Trade receivables days [24.9]

Payables days [   ]

11.13 Which one of the following transactions will affect the overall amount of working capital?

○ Receipt of the full amount of cash from a trade receivable

○ Payment of an account payable

○ Sale of a non-current asset on credit at its carrying amount ⁻

○ Purchase of inventory on credit

11.14 FUM Co has a current ratio of 2. Trade receivables are $3 million and current liabilities are $2 million.

Calculate inventory days if cost of sales are $10 million per annum and FUM Co has a zero cash balance. Assume a 365-day year and give your answer to one decimal place.

[_____] days.　　　　　　　✓

11.15 Select the appropriate box to denote whether the following statements concerning working capital management are true or false.

	True	False
Working capital should increase as sales increase.	☐	☐
An increase in the working capital/cash operating cycle will decrease profitability.	☐	☐
Overtrading is also known as undercapitalisation.	☐	☐

---

12 Receivables, payables and inventory

12.1 Which of the following services is LEAST LIKELY to be offered by a factoring company?

○ Provision of finance by advancing, say, 80% of invoice value immediately, and the remainder on settlement of the debt by the customer

○ Taking over responsibility for administration of the client's sales ledger

○ Deciding what credit limits customers should be given

○ Without recourse finance, ie taking over responsibility for irrecoverable debts

---

12.2 Which one of the following is NOT a stage in the credit cycle?

○ Negotiation of the price of the goods

○ Receipt of the customer order

○ Checking the credit limit

○ Goods despatched with delivery note

12.3 Which of the following sentences best describes invoice discounting?

○ Reducing or discounting the amount owed by a customer in order to ensure payment

○ Writing off a debt because the customer is not expected to pay

○ Selling invoices to a finance company that then collects the cash from the customer

○ Selling invoices to a finance company for less than their face value while continuing to collect the cash from the customer

12.4 Which of the following would NEVER be considered a feature of factoring?

○ The factoring company charges a fee for its services.

○ Interest is charged on the amount advanced to the client from the date of the advance until the debt is settled by the client's customer.

○ The factoring company advances a percentage of the invoice value immediately, with the remainder being paid when the client's customer settles the debt.

○ The borrowing is repayable over a number of years.

12.5 If an entity regularly fails to pay its suppliers by the normal due dates, it may lead to a number of problems.

Which TWO of the following problems could result from exceeding suppliers' trade credit terms?

☐ Having insufficient cash to pay debts as they fall due

☐ Difficulty in obtaining credit from new suppliers

☐ Reduction in credit rating

☐ Exceeding the bank's overdraft limit

12.6 Z Co is considering selling its receivables to a debt factor.

The debt factor will pay 90% of the value of invoices finally paid with the balance kept as their service charge. Z Co normally gets 40% of the amount invoiced within 30 days. 80% of the remaining balance is usually received after 60 days with the remaining 20% written off as irrecoverable.

The debt factor tends to suffer irrecoverable debts amounting to $10 in every $100 invoiced.

If Z Co sells its debts to the debt factor, by how much will cash flow change for every $100 factored?

90 × 81

○ $2 increase

○ $1 increase   40

◉ $7 decrease   32

○ $8 decrease   48

12.7 Which ONE of the following statements best describes the invoice discounting service offered by a factoring company?

   ○   The factoring company takes over the administration of the client's invoicing system.

   ○   The factoring company enforces the correct administration of the client's system of offering cash discounts and ensures that discounts are disallowed in line with policy.

   ○   The factoring company advances finance to the client against the debts which the factor has purchased – up to 80% of the value of the debts.

   ○   The factoring company purchases a selection of invoices at a discount, thus providing the client with a source of short-term finance.

12.8 Which THREE of the following services does a factor most commonly offer?

   ☐   Administration of the client's payables ledger department

   ☐   Provision of finance against the client's outstanding receivables

   ☐   Protection against irrecoverable debts

   ☐   Administration of the client's invoicing and debt collection

   ☐   Provision of credit rating information for prospective customers

---

12.9 A company is offering its customers the choice of a cash discount of 3% for payment within 15 days of the invoice date or paying in full within 45 days.

What is the effective annual interest rate of the cash discount?

   ○   43.3%

   ○   12.5%

   ○   44.9%

   ○   24.7%

12.10 DEN is considering whether to factor its sales ledger. It has been offered a 'without-recourse' package by the factor at a cost of 2% sales, plus an administration fee of $5,000 per year. Annual sales are currently $1 million, with irrecoverable debts of 1%.

What is the annual cost of the package to DEN likely to be?

   ○ $5,000

   ○ $20,000

   ○ $24,800

   ○ $25,000

12.11 GOR is considering changing its credit policy. It currently allows customers 90 days' credit, but suffers irrecoverable debts amounting to 3% of its annual sales of $2 million. It is proposing to reduce the credit period to 30 days, which should cause the irrecoverable debts to fall to 1% of turnover. However, it expects that this will result in a reduction in sales of 20%. This reduction will also be reflected in the level of purchases and inventory holding.

GOR's current figures are as follows:

Inventories (raw materials and finished goods)	$500,000
Annual purchases	$360,000
Payables	$30,000
Cost of capital	10%

What will be the effect of its new credit policy on the annual financing cost?

- ○ Saving of $46,000
- ○ Increase of $46,000
- ○ Saving of $36,000
- ○ Increase of $36,000

12.12 CD uses factoring to manage its trade receivables. The factor advances 80% of invoiced sales and charges interest at a rate of 12% per annum. CD has estimated sales revenue for next year of $2,190,000. The average time for the factor to receive payment from customers is 50 days.

What will be the estimated interest charge payable to the factor for the next year?

- ○ $28,800
- ○ $262,800
- ○ $210,240
- ○ $36,000

12.13 AB entity has trade payables at the year end of $23,000. AB's cost of sales for the year are $103,628, opening inventory was $8,000 and closing inventory at the year end is $12,000. All purchases are on credit.

Calculate the trade payable days ratio:

	days

12.14 NC enjoys a 60-day credit period from all of its suppliers and has the following trade payables report:

Account number	Supplier name	Balance $	Up to 30 days $	31–60 days $	61–90 days $	Over 90 days $
100378	X Co	250	50	200	–	–
100507	Y Co	1,000	–	–	–	1,000
103249	Z Co	750	150	300	300	–
Total		2,000	200	500	300	1,000
Percentage		100%	10%	25%	15%	50%

Which TWO of the following statements are NOT true?

☐ The debt to Y Co is more than 90 days old and there may be a loss of goodwill.

☑ X Co will be dissatisfied with what NC owes it.

☐ Overall NC is very good at paying suppliers within due dates.

☐ The amount owed to Z Co after the allowable credit period is $300.

☐ The table is called an 'aged analysis' table.

12.15 **Which one of the following is NOT considered to be a cost of holding inventory?**

⊘ Loss of goodwill as a result of being unable to complete customer orders due to lack of inventory

○ Insurance cost of inventory

○ Storage cost of inventory

○ Interest lost on cash invested in inventory

12.16 The economic order quantity (EOQ) can be expressed as follows:

$$EOQ = \sqrt{\frac{2C_oD}{C_h}}$$

What does Ch describe in this formula?

⊘ The cost of holding one unit of inventory for one year

○ The cost of placing one order

○ The cost of a unit of inventory

○ The customer demand for the item

12.17 Create Co requires 20,000 units of a certain component every year. The purchase price per unit is $40 and it costs $64 to place and receive delivery of an order irrespective of its size. Create Co's cost of capital is 10% per annum.

Create Co currently places orders for 800 units, although a discount scheme for larger orders exists which works as follows.

Minimum order quantity	Discount rate
1,000	1%
4,000	2%
8,000	3%

What size of order should Create Co place if its aim is to minimise costs?

○ 800 units

○ 1,000 units

○ 4,000 units

○ 8,000 units

12.18   Which of the following can the economic order quantity model be used to determine?

(1)   The order quantity
(2)   The buffer inventory
(3)   The re-order level

○   1 and 3 only

○   1 and 2 only   ✓

○   2 and 3 only

◉   1 only

12.19   JD is a retailer of storage boxes. Annual demand is 39,000 units spread evenly throughout the year. Ordering costs are $100 per order and the cost of holding one storage box in inventory for one year is $1.60. It takes two weeks for an order to be delivered to JD's premises.

What is the economic order quantity (EOQ) for the storage boxes?

$$EOQ = \sqrt{\frac{2C_oD}{C_h}}$$

○   1,746 units

◉   2,208 units   ✓

○   2,793 units

○   1,248 units

12.20   JD is a retailer of storage boxes. Annual demand is 39,000 units spread evenly throughout the year. Ordering costs are $100 per order and the cost of holding one storage box in inventory for one year is $1.60. It takes two weeks for an order to be delivered to JD's premises.

The reorder level that would ensure that JD never runs out of inventory of storage boxes is:

○   1,560 units

○   4,416 units

○   3,492 units

◉   1,500 units   ✓

13   Managing cash

13.1   EX is preparing its cash forecast for the next three months.

Which ONE of the following items should be left out of its calculations?

○   Expected gain on the disposal of a piece of land

○   Tax payment due that relates to last year's profits

○   Rental payment on a leased vehicle

○   Receipt of a new bank loan raised for the purpose of purchasing new machinery

13.2 AB is preparing its cash budget for next year. The accounts receivable at the beginning of next year are expected to be $460,000. The budgeted sales are $5,400,000 and will occur evenly throughout the year. 80% of the budgeted sales will be on credit and the remainder will be cash sales. Credit customers pay in the month following sale.

What are the budgeted cash receipts from customers next year?

  ○ $5,040,000

  ○ $5,410,000

  ○ $5,500,000

  ○ $4,420,000

13.3 Claw is preparing its cash flow forecast for the next quarter.

Which of the following items should be excluded from the cash flow forecast?

  ○   The receipt of a bank loan that has been raised for the purpose of investment in a new rolling mill

  ○   Depreciation of the new rolling mill

  ○   A tax payment that is due to be made which relates to profits earned in a previous accounting period

  ○   Disposal proceeds from the sale of the old rolling mill

---

13.4 BC had trade receivables of $242,000 at the start of the year. BC forecasts that the sales revenue for the year will be $1,500,000. All sales are on credit.

Trade receivable days at the end of the year are expected to be 60 days based on a 365-day year.

What are the expected receipts from customers during the year?

  ○ $1,495,425

  ○ $1,742,000

  ○ $1,253,425

  ○ $1,504,575

13.5 DY's trade receivables balance at 1 April 20X6 was $22,000. DY's income statement showed revenue from credit sales of $290,510 during the year ended 31 March 20X7.

DY's trade receivables days at 31 March 20X7 were 49 days.

Assume DY's sales occur evenly throughout the year and that all balances outstanding at 1 April 20X6 have been received.

Also, assume all sales are on credit, there were no irrecoverable debts and no trade discount was given.

How much cash did DY receive from its customers during the year to 31 March 20X7?

  ○ $268,510

  ○ $273,510

  ○ $312,510

  ○ $351,510

13.6 A management accountant has prepared part of a company's budget for the next six months.

	Balances at 31 March (actual)	Balances at 30 September (budgeted)
	$	$
Raw materials trade payables	58,000	47,000
Closing inventory of raw materials	39,000	51,000

The budget for the cost of raw materials used in the six-month period to 30 September is $372,000.

Calculate the cash required to pay the raw materials trade payables for the period ended 30 September. Give your answer to the nearest $.

$	

13.7 Moon, a printing business, has annual sales of $1.1 million and a gross profit margin of 50%. It is currently experiencing short-term cash flow difficulties, and intends to delay its payments to trade suppliers by one month.

Assume that sales are spread evenly over the year and inventory levels remain constant throughout.

Calculate the amount by which the cash balance will benefit in the short term from this change in policy. Give your answer to the nearest $.

$	

13.8 Fenton Co's projected revenue for 20X1 is $50,000.

It is forecast that 25% of sales will occur in January and the remaining sales will be earned equally among the remaining 11 months. All sales are on credit.

Customers' accounts are settled 55% in the month of sale and 40% in the following month. 5% of sales are written off as irrecoverable debts after two months.

Calculate the estimated receipts for March. Give your answer to the nearest $.

$	

13.9 Toaster Co is a trading company that does not hold any inventory.

Each month the following relationships hold:

Gross profit   25% of sales

Closing trade payables   15% of cost of sales

Sales are expected to be $40,000 in April and $48,000 in May.

How much will Toaster Co pay to its suppliers in May? Give your answer to the nearest $.

$ [   ]

13.10 **Which one of the following statements about an overdraft facility is correct?**

- ○ An overdraft is a permanent loan.
- ○ Assets are always required as security.
- ○ Interest is paid on the full facility.
- ○ Compared with other types of loan it is quick and easy to set up.

13.11 **Which of the following is NOT a form of short-term investment?**

- ○ Treasury bills
- ○ Trade receivable factoring
- ○ Local authority bonds
- ○ Bank deposits

13.12 **Which of the following is NOT a form of short-term finance?**

- ○ Bank overdraft
- ○ Credit from trade payables
- ○ Bank loans less than six months
- ○ Treasury bills

13.13 **Which of the following is an advantage for an entity of securing an overdraft rather than a short-term fixed-interest loan?**

- ○ Budgeting for cash is easier with an overdraft.
- ○ An overdraft is technically repayable on demand.
- ○ The entity's cash flows are more certain with the overdraft.
- ○ The terms of an overdraft are more easily changed to accommodate different needs within the entity.

13.14 **Which of the following methods could NOT be used to reduce the risks of irrecoverable debts when trading overseas?**

- ○ Export factoring
- ○ Forfaiting
- ○ Advances against collections
- ○ Documentary credits

13.15 Which of the following is NOT a method used for raising finance to fund export sales?

- ○ Bills of exchange
- ○ Credit insurance
- ○ Documentary credits
- ○ Countertrade

13.16 Which of the following statements about bond rates are true?

(1) The coupon rate determines the amount of interest received annually.

(2) The yield to maturity is the discount rate that should be used to discount the amounts received.

- ○ Both statements are false.
- ○ Both statements are true.
- ○ Statement 1 is true and statement 2 is false.
- ○ Statement 1 is false and statement 2 is true.

13.17 KEN is awaiting the go-ahead to start its new building programme. This is likely to take place within the next 90 days, but the precise start date and timing of the cash flows are still uncertain. The company has $150,000 available in cash in anticipation of the investment.

Which of the following is the LEAST appropriate use of the funds in the interim period?

- ○ Investment in equities
- ○ Treasury bills
- ○ Bank deposits
- ○ Local authority deposits

13.18 Which one of the following MOST appropriately describes forfaiting?

- ○ It is a method of providing medium-term export finance.
- ○ It provides long-term finance to importers.
- ○ It provides equity finance for the redemption of shares.
- ○ It is the surrender of a share because of the failure to make a payment on a partly-paid share.

13.19 Which of the following statements about certificates of deposit is FALSE?

- ○ Certificates of deposit are negotiable instruments issued by banks.
- ○ Certificates of deposit will typically have maturity periods of between three and five years.
- ○ Certificates of deposit are non-negotiable.
- ○ Certificates of deposit are issued in bearer form.

13.20 **Which of the following statements best describes a documentary credit?**

○ A negotiable instrument, drawn by one party on another, who by signing the document acknowledges the debt, which may be payable immediately or at some future date

○ A document issued by a bank on behalf of a customer authorising a person to draw money to a specified amount from its branches or correspondents, usually in another country, when the conditions set out in the document have been met

○ A series of promissory notes, guaranteed by a highly rated international bank, and purchased at a discount to face value by an exporter's bank

○ A form of export finance where the debt is sold to a factor, at a discount, in return for prompt cash

Answers to objective test questions

1 Regulatory environment and corporate governance

1.1 The correct answer is: IFRS Interpretations Committee.

Guidance on application and interpretation of IFRSs is provided by the IFRS Interpretations Committee.

1.2 The correct answer is: IFRS Foundation Trustees.

The IFRS Foundation Trustees are responsible for governance and fundraising, and publish an annual report on the IASB's activities. The Trustees also review annually the strategy of the IASB and its effectiveness.

1.3 The correct answer is: IFRS Advisory Council.

1.4 The correct answer is: A system by which companies are directed and controlled.

All the other options are aspects of corporate governance but none provides a precise definition.

1.5 The correct answer is: The nomination committee should consist entirely of executive directors.

Corporate governance practice varies, but the UK Corporate Governance Code recommends that the majority of nomination committee members should be independent non-executive directors.

1.6 The correct answer is: Priority given to different user groups in different countries.

1.7 The correct answer is: Rotation of lead audit partner every five years.

1.8 The correct answer is: IFRS Interpretations Committee.

The IFRS Foundation is the parent entity of the IASB, and the IFRS Advisory Committee advises the IASB on major standard-setting projects.

1.9 The correct answers are:

- Approving the annual budget of the IASB
- Reviewing the strategy of the IASB and its effectiveness
- Appointing members of the IASB, the IFRS Interpretations Committee and the IFRS Advisory Council

The IFRS Foundation Trustees are also responsible for establishing and amending the operating procedures, consultative arrangements and due process for the IASB, the Interpretations Committee, and the Advisory Council.

1.10 The correct answers are:

- It can be applied across different legal jurisdictions.
- It can stress those areas where rules cannot easily be applied.
- It puts the emphasis on investors making up their own minds.

Adherence to standards and definite targets are characteristics of a rules-based approach, although many codes that are largely based on principles might include some targets.

1.11 The correct answers are:

- It emphasises measurable achievements by companies.
- It can easily be applied in jurisdictions where the letter of the law is stressed.

A rules-based approach implies that companies must comply and do not have the option of explaining non-compliance. Rulebooks cannot normally cover all eventualities, meaning a rules-based approach may have difficulty coping with situations that are not covered by the rulebook. A rules-based approach can be difficult to apply across different legal jurisdictions, because the rulebook will have to be compatible with variations in local law.

1.12 The correct answer is: The audit firm giving evidence in court on behalf of the client.

1.13   The correct answer is: Recruiting senior management for the client.

Recruiting senior management for the client is a possible source of threat to independence.

1.14   The correct answer is: Auditing financial statements.

The audit of the financial statements will be carried out by an accountant in practice.

1.15   The correct answer is: Reliability.

The other fundamental principles are professional behaviour and professional competence and due care.

1.16   The correct answer is: Professional competence and due care, Confidentiality, Integrity.

Reliability, morality and efficiency are not fundamental principles.

1.17   The correct answer is: Self-interest.

If such threats are significant (ie the interest is direct and of high value), safeguards will have to be put in place.

1.18   The correct answer is: Professional competence and due care.

This raises issues of professional competence and due care. You know that you do not have the knowledge to answer these questions at this time and in this situation. For your own professional safety, you should make the client clearly aware of this and not be prepared to give any opinion, as this may be relied upon by the client despite the circumstances. The most appropriate form of action would be to make an appointment with the client to discuss the matter properly after you have done some research into these specific areas, or refer them to a colleague with experience in this area.

1.19   The correct answer is: It encourages compliance by requiring a professional person to actively consider the issues.

The other statements all describe the features of a rules-based code.

1.20   The correct answer is: Disclosure of information to advance the interests of a new client.

This would not be permitted under the Code.

2   The *Conceptual Framework*

2.1   The correct answer is: It is an accounting standard that companies have to comply with.

The IASB's *Conceptual Framework for Financial Reporting* is not an accounting standard; however, it is extremely influential for companies preparing and presenting their financial statements.

2.2   The correct answer is: Profits.

The *Conceptual Framework* defines the elements as the broad classes into which the effect of transactions and other events are categorised in the financial statements.

An asset is a present economic resource controlled by the entity as a result of past events.

A liability is a present obligation of the entity to transfer an economic resource as a result of past events.

Equity is the residual interest in the assets of the entity after deducting all its liabilities.

2.3   The correct answers are:

- Similar items should be treated in the same way from one period to the next.

- Similar items within a single set of financial statements should be given similar accounting treatment.

These statements describe comparability.

Under accrual accounting, the non-cash effects of transactions should be reflected in the financial statements for the accounting period in which they occur and not in the period where any cash involved is received or paid.

Information is relevant if it has a predictive and/or confirmatory value.

2.4   The correct answer is: It provides a framework for the formulation of accounting standards.

2.5   The correct answers are:

- It can suggest solutions to difficult issues whilst ensuring a consistent approach.
- It helps to reduce the scope for individual judgement and potential subjectivity.
- It demands that financial statements contain relevant information.

It helps ensure that solutions to different issues are the right ones and are consistently applied. It provides guidance in areas not subject to accounting standards, which will help make different financial statements more comparable.

This may mean that the legal form of transaction is superseded by the substance of the transaction as required by IAS 1 *Presentation of Financial Statements*.

Although the *Framework* document is similar to the US Statement of Principles (issued by FASB in the US) it is not the same. Also, not all the US GAAP rules are consistent with the US Statement of Principles.

2.6   The correct answers are:

- Information that is free from error
- Information that is complete

Information is material if it has the ability to influence decisions. Materiality relates to the fundamental qualitative characteristic of relevance rather than faithful representation.

Verification is an enhancing qualitative characteristic.

2.7   The correct answers are:

- Accrual accounting
- Faithful representation
- Relevance

The underlying assumption is going concern.

2.8   The correct answers are:

- Accounting standards will develop in a more coherent fashion.

- Different accounting presentations of transactions not currently covered by an IAS/IFRS should reduce.

The technical content of new standards is becoming ever more demanding. Implementation problems will always remain. A conceptual framework can never make development easier or implementation more acceptable. It should, however, mean that standards are more coherent as a body of principles/rules.

This coherence and common use of definitions and principles should also reduce confusing different presentations where no accounting standard currently exists.

2.9   The correct answer is: Neutrality.

This ensures that the financial statements are free from bias and will therefore more closely reflect the activities of the entity throughout the period.

2.10   The correct answers are:

- It assists those preparing financial statements in developing consistent accounting policies where an IFRS allows a choice of accounting policy.

- It assists the Board of the IASB in the development of future International Financial Reporting Standards and in its review of existing standards.

The purpose of the *Conceptual Framework* is to:

- Assist the IASB to develop International Financial Reporting Standards (IFRSs) that are based on **consistent concepts;**

- Assist those preparing financial statements to develop consistent accounting policies **where no IFRS applies** to a particular transaction or when an IFRS allows a choice of accounting policy; and

- Assist all parties to understand and interpret IFRSs.

A conceptual framework helps to provide clarity on the fundamental principles governing the preparation and presentation of financial statements; however, it does not ensure compliance with local legislation and it cannot prevent misleading financial statements just as traffic laws don't stop people speeding.

2.11   The correct answers are:

- Relevance
- Faithful representation

Relevance and faithful representation are fundamental qualitative characteristics of financial information.

Predictive value is a subsection of relevance.

Comparability and understandability are two of the four enhancing qualitative characteristics of financial information. The other two are verifiability and timeliness.

Consistency is a subsection of comparability.

2.12   The correct answer is: To provide information about the reporting entity that is useful to a variety of users.

The other options are implicitly included in this.

2.13   The correct answer is: A present obligation of the entity to transfer an economic resource as a result of past events.

This is the definition of a liability according to the *Conceptual Framework*.

2.14   The correct answer is: An entity that is required, or chooses, to prepare financial statements.

A reporting entity does not have to be a legal entity or a group.

Two or more entities not linked by a parent–subsidiary relationship is the definition of a combined entity.

2.15   The correct answer is: Fair value.

The following definitions are found in the *Conceptual Framework*.

The historical cost of an asset is the costs incurred in acquiring/creating the asset plus transactions costs.

Value in use is the present value of the cash flows, or other economic benefits, that an entity expects to derive from the use of an asset and from its ultimate disposal.

The current cost of an asset is the cost of an equivalent asset at the measurement date (consideration that would be paid plus transaction costs).

3 Non-current assets

3.1 The correct answers are:

- Directly attributable labour costs
- A reasonable proportion of indirect costs
- Interest on capital borrowed to finance production of the asset

Labour costs directly attributable to producing the asset are part of its total cost of production.

Production costs may include a reasonable proportion of indirect costs.

Interest incurred on capital borrowed to finance production of the asset is a relevant production cost when a company is constructing an asset for its own consumption.

3.2 The correct answers are:

- For a purchased asset, expenses incidental (directly attributable) to the acquisition of the asset
- For a manufactured asset, direct costs of production plus a reasonable proportion of indirect costs

For a purchased asset, expenses incidental to the acquisition of the asset and the direct costs and a reasonable proportion of the indirect costs of a manufactured asset can be included in the calculation of the cost of a non-current asset.

3.3 The correct answer is:

- Dr Accumulated depreciation $20,000, Dr Property at cost $30,000; Cr Revaluation surplus $50,000

DEBIT	Accumulated depreciation	$20,000	
DEBIT	Property at cost	$30,000	
CREDIT	Revaluation surplus		$50,000

All depreciation to date must be eliminated.

The original cost is increased to the revalued amount.

3.4 The correct answer is: A method that allocates the depreciable amount as fairly as possible.

IAS 16 does not prescribe any specific method.

3.5 The correct answer is: $38,000.

CA (30 September 20X6)	= 40,000	
	= 80%	
CA (30 September 20X5)	= (40,000 × 100)/80	
	= 50,000	
CA (30 September 20X4)	= (50,000 × 100)/80	
	= 62,500	
Cost (1 October 20X3)	= (62,500 × 100)/80	
	= 78,125	
Accumulated depreciation	= $78,125 – $40,000	
	= $38,000	

3.6   The correct answers are:

- Freehold buildings
- Plant and machinery

Buildings and plant and machinery have a finite useful life and are thus depreciated in accordance with IAS 16 *Property, Plant and Equipment*.

Freehold land has an indefinite life and is not depreciated.

Investments are not depreciated but are subject to specific valuation rules.

3.7   The correct answer is: Shares in another company held as a short-term store of spare cash.

As the shares are held for the short term, they would be classified as a current asset investment.

Both types of freehold property are being held on a continuing basis and so are classified as tangible non-current assets.

A limited edition delivery van used in the entity's operations is also a tangible non-current asset.

3.8   The correct answer is: Initial operating losses while the production plant reaches planned performance.

Per IAS 16, this should be treated as an expense, not part of an asset. The other costs are all directly attributable to bringing the asset into operation. As the production plant must be dismantled at the end of the lease, the costs of dismantling are included.

3.9   The correct answer is: Capitalised and depreciated over the period to the next inspection.

The cost should not be accrued for or provided for. The inspection is treated as an additional component, so it is capitalised and depreciated.

3.10   The correct answer is: $31,600.

This is calculated as:

	$
Original purchase price	50,000
Depreciation 20X1 ([50,000 – 5,000]/5)	(9,000)
Depreciation 20X2	(9,000)
Upgrade	15,000
	47,000
Depreciation 20X3 ([47,000 – 5,000]/5)	(8,400)
Carrying amount 1 January 20X4	38,600
Disposal proceeds	(7,000)
Loss on disposal	31,600

3.11   The correct answer is: $1,055,000.

	$
Purchase price	780,000
Import duties	117,000
Site preparation costs	30,000
Installation costs	28,000
Estimated cost of dismantling and removal of the asset, required to be recognised as a provision	100,000
	1,055,000

3.12   The correct answer is: An allocation of EW's administration costs, based on EW staff time spent on the construction as a percentage of the total staff time.

Administration costs would not be included as these do not relate specifically to the non-current asset.

3.13   The correct answer is: $4,896.

	$
Cost 1.4.X2	10,000
Depreciation to 1.10.X3 (18 months straight line)	(1,500)
Carrying amount at 1.10.X3	8,500
Depreciation to 1.10.X4 (20%)	(1,700)
Carrying amount at 1.10.X4	6,800
Depreciation to 1.10.X5 (20%)	(1,360)
Carrying amount at 1.10.X5	5,440
Depreciation to 31.3.X6 (20% × 6/12)	(544)
Carrying amount at 31.3.X6	4,896

3.14   The correct answer is: $5,040.

	$
Cost at 1.1.X1	40,000
Depreciation to 31.12.X3 ([40,000 – 4,000] × 3/10)	(10,800)
Carrying amount at 31.12.X3	29,200
Residual value	(4,000)
	25,200
Depreciation for y/e 31.12.X4 (25,200/5 years)	5,040

3.15 The correct answer is: $150,000

	$	$
Proceeds of disposal		1,100,000
Carrying amount at 1.1.X6	960,000	
Depreciation ([960,000/48] × 6/12)	(10,000)	
Carrying amount at 1.7.X6		(950,000)
Gain on disposal		150,000

The amount in the revaluation surplus in respect of the building will now be transferred to retained earnings, but is not recognised in profit for the year. This transfer is shown in the statement of changes in equity.

4 Leases

4.1 The correct answer is: $5,716.

		$
1.4.X3	Present value of future lease payments	15,600
1.4.X3–31.3.X4	Finance cost (interest at 8%)	1,248
31.3.X4	Instalment 1	(6,000)
31.3.X4	Liability c/d 31 March 20X4	10,848
1.4.X4–31.3.X5	Finance cost (interest at 8%)	868
31.3.X5	Instalment 2	(6,000)
31.3.X5	Non-current liability	5,716

4.2 The correct answers are:

- The lessee obtains the right to use an asset in exchange for consideration.
- The asset cannot be substituted by the lessor.

A lease contract must relate to an identified asset.

If the lessor retains the right to direct the use of the asset, the lessee has not obtained right of use.

4.3 The correct answer is: $1,068,000.

	$
Initial measurement of lease liability (present value of future lease payments)	900,000
Lease payments made at/before commencement date (deposit)	100,000
Initial direct costs incurred by the lessee	28,000
Decommissioning costs	40,000
	1,068,000

4.4 The correct answer is: Deducted from the initial measurement of the right-of-use asset.

4.5 The correct answer is: $600,000.

As ownership is expected to be transferred, the asset is depreciated over its useful life of eight years and so the annual depreciation is calculated as $800,000/8 years = $100,000.

The asset will have been held for two years at 31 December 20X5.

4.6 The correct answer is: $45,000.

		$
1.4.X7	Initial measurement of liability (present value of future lease payments)	118,000
1.4.X7–31.3.X8	Interest at 7%	8,260
31.3.X8	Liability c/d at 31 March 20X8	126,260
1.4.X8	Instalment 2	(45,000)
	Non-current liability	81,260

4.7 The correct answers are:

- PYM Co has leased a machine for $3,000 a month for 18 months.
- WVX Co has leased a car for $5,000 a year for four years.

TDK Co has entered into a short-term lease (less than 12 months).

ADV Co is leasing a low value item.

These arrangements can both be covered by the IFRS 16 exemption.

4.8 The correct answer is: From the commencement of the lease to the earlier of the end of the lease term and the end of the useful life of the vehicle.

4.9 The correct answer is: $3,840.

$1,440 × 8/9 = $1,280 per month

$1,280 × 3 months = $3,840

4.10 The correct answer is: $407

		$
1.7.X6	Present value of future lease payments	10,500
1.7.X6–30.6.X7	Finance cost (10,500 × 7%)	735
30.6.X7	Instalment paid	(3,000)
30.6.X7	Liability c/d	8,235
1.7.X7–30.6.X8	Finance cost (8,235 × 7%)	576
30.6.X8	Instalment paid	(3,000)
30.6.X8	Liability c/d	5,811
1.7.X8–30.6.X9	Finance cost (5,811 × 7%)	407

4.11 The correct answer is: $49,400

	$
Finance cost (160,000 × 9%)	14,400
Depreciation ([50,000 + 160,000]/6 years)	35,000
	49,400

The lease liability is calculated as the present value of lease payments not paid at the commencement date which is $160,000 and it is this value on which interest will be incurred.

BPP
LEARNING
MEDIA

The right-of-use asset is measured at the present value of the lease payments not paid at the commencement date of $160,000 plus the value of the lease payments made at or before the commencement date. Here this is the first instalment of $50,000 because instalments are paid in advance. As the option to extend is likely to be taken up, the asset is depreciated over six years, being the initial lease term of four years plus the additional extension period of two years.

4.12   The correct answer is: $90,000.

	$
Present value of future lease payments	85,000
Lease payments made at/before commencement date (deposit)	7,000
Initial direct costs incurred by the lessee	3,000
Lease incentive received	(5,000)
	90,000

4.13   The correct answer is: $26,000.

	$
Finance costs (75,000 × 8%)	6,000
Depreciation ([75,000 + 5,000]/4 years)	20,000
	26,000

4.14   The correct answer is: $100,000.

	$
Initial measurement of lease liability	74,000
Lease payments made at/before commencement date	14,000
Decommissioning cost	12,000
	100,000

4.15   The correct answers are:

- Depreciation charge for the year in respect of right-of-use assets
- Interest expense on lease liabilities

IFRS 16 *Leases* asks for the carrying amount of right-of-use assets, not their fair value. There is no requirement in respect of lease incentives.

5   Other accounting standards

5.1   The correct answer is: The operating performance of the machine has declined.

Market values and technological changes are external factors. The machine being fully depreciated does not mean it is impaired.

5.2   The correct answer is: $22,000.

The recoverable amount is the higher of the value in use of the asset and the asset's fair value less costs of disposal (ie the net realisable value of the asset).

5.3   The correct answer is:

$200,000   Recognise in other comprehensive income

On 30 September 20X4 the building was revalued upwards by $900,000 and the gain on revaluation was taken to the revaluation surplus:

Revaluation surplus at 30 September 20X4 = $1.8m − ($1m − ($1m × 2/20))

= $900,000

Therefore IAS 36 *Impairment of Assets* states that the impairment loss of $200,000 ($1.7m − $1.5m) should be charged against the previous revaluation surplus of $900,000 leaving a revaluation surplus of $700,000 and a carrying amount for the building of $1,500,000.

Carrying amount of building at 30 September 20X5 = $1.8m − ($1.8m/18)

= $1.7m

Market value at 30 Sept 20X5 = $1.5m

5.4   The correct answer is: $0.

The recoverable amount of the machine (higher of fair value less costs of disposal and value in use) is $150,000. This is higher than the carrying amount so the machine is not impaired.

5.5   The correct answer is: $1,500.

The carrying amount of the machine at 30 September 20X5 is $10,500 ($21,000/6 years × 3 years).

The recoverable amount of the asset at 30 September 20X5 is $9,000. This is the higher of the asset's fair value less costs of disposal ($9,200 − $500) and its value in use ($9,000).

Therefore the impairment loss is $1,500 ($10,500 − $9,000).

5.6   The correct answer is: $730,000.

The asset should be classified as held for sale and valued at the lower of its carrying amount ($750,000) and its fair value less costs of disposal ($740,000 − $10,000).

Note that non-current assets held for sale are not depreciated.

5.7   The correct answer is: Disclose the machine separately from other property, plant and equipment and no longer depreciate it.

The machine will be presented under non-current assets held for sale.

5.8   The correct answer is: $370 million.

The airline operation was sold before the year end and was a distinguishable component of the entity and is therefore a discontinued operation as defined by IFRS 5 *Non-current Assets Held for Sale and Discontinued Operations*.

A separate line in the statement of profit or loss and other comprehensive income for discontinued operations should be included after the profit after tax for continuing operations. IFRS 5 states that this should be made up of the post-tax profit or loss of the discontinued operation ($100 million) and the post-tax gain or loss on disposal of the airline assets. The loss on sale of the fleet of aircraft of $250 million and the provision for severance payments of $20 million will both be reported in this line.

The $10 million costs relating to the restructuring will be reported as part of the continuing activities, probably as part of administrative expenses. They are not included within the amount for discontinued operations.

5.9   The correct answer is: $45,000.

The assets of the manufacturing division should be valued at the lower of the carrying amount and the fair value less costs of disposal.

For YS this is the lower of $443,000 and $398,000 ($423,000 − $25,000) and so an impairment loss of $45,000 should be recognised.

5.10 The correct answer is: $12,000.

The scenario provides the carrying amounts of the assets at the beginning of the period, ie at 31 March 20X0. The outlet was classified as held for sale on 31 March 20X1 and so the assets need to be depreciated for the period from 1 April 20X0 to 31 March 20X1.

This is calculated as:

	Carrying amount at 1 April 20X0 $'000	Dep'n charge for 20X1 $'000	Carrying amount at 31 March 20X1 $'000
Land (no depreciation)	150	0	150
Buildings	20	40 (cost) × 5% = 2	18
Plant and equipment	25	25(CA) × 20% = 5	20
	195		188

Therefore the assets have a carrying amount of $188,000 at 31 March 20X1.

When they are classified as held for sale they must be valued at the lower of the current carrying amount ($188,000) and the fair value less costs of disposal ($176,000).

Therefore there is an impairment loss of $12,000 ($188,000 – $176,000).

5.11 The correct answers are:

- The sale or closure must be completed by the end of the reporting period.
- The anticipated sale is an associate acquired exclusively with a view to resale.

The sale or closure does not have to occur by the year end for the operation to be treated as discontinued.

A discontinued operation can be a subsidiary acquired exclusively with a view to resale, not an associate.

5.12 The correct answers are:

- Carriage inwards on raw materials delivered to factory
- Factory supervisors' salaries
- Factory heating and lighting
- Import duties on raw materials

Carriage outwards is charged to distribution and abnormal costs are not included in inventory.

5.13 The correct answer is: $8,500.

According to IAS 2, inventory should be valued at the lower of cost and net realisable value, so $8,500.

Cost	$	Net realisable value	$
Direct material ($3 × 1,000)	3,000	Selling price ($30 × 1,000)	30,000
Direct labour ($4 × 1,000)	4,000	Gross profit margin	×50%
		Wholesale price	15,000
Total direct costs	7,000	Trade discount	–30%
Factory overhead ($100,000 × 2%)	2,000	Net sales value	10,500
Total cost	9,000	Selling costs ($2 × 1,000)	(2,000)
		Net realisable value	8,500

5.14   The correct answers are:

- Physical deterioration of inventory
- Increases in the cost of raw materials
- Errors in production or purchasing

Physical deterioration of inventory would mean that goods might well not realise as much as it originally cost to buy or produce them.

Increases in cost may well mean that the margin of sales price over cost has been eroded away.

Errors in purchasing might mean that the goods will not realise the selling price originally budgeted. The most extreme case of this is goods becoming obsolete.

An increase in selling price of goods sold would increase net realisable value.

5.15   The correct answer is: The treatment is acceptable provided only production related overheads are included using a normal basis of activity to calculate the absorption rates.

Only production overheads can be included in value of inventory.

5.16   The correct answers are:

- Average cost calculates a new weighted average cost upon each delivery.
- FIFO assumes that inventory is used in the order in which it is delivered.

Replacement cost is valuing inventory at the current cost of acquisition – ie how much it would cost to replace the inventory you have today.

Inventory may be valued using standard cost provided that the standard cost is kept up to date.

The net realisable value is calculated on selling price less costs of completion of the inventory items which are yet to be incurred, less any selling costs. NRV should be used if this figure is less than the cost of inventory, therefore this is also incorrect.

5.17   The correct answers are:

- The $150,000 dividend was shown in the notes to the financial statements at 31 October 20X5.
- The dividend is shown as a deduction in the statement of changes in equity for the year ended 31 October 20X6.

The dividend was not declared before 31 October 20X5 and so cannot be recognised during that year. Instead it should be disclosed in a note to the financial statements at 31 October 20X5.

The dividend will be recognised in the statement of changes in equity in the year ended 31 October 20X6.

5.18   The correct answers are:

- Opening new trading operations
- Announcement of plan to discontinue an operation
- Expropriation (seizure) of major assets by government

An adjusting event is an event that provides further evidence of a condition that already existed at the reporting date.

A non-adjusting event relates to the situation where the condition did not exist at the reporting date.

5.19   The correct answer is: $1,664,000.

This is calculated as:

	$
Profit before tax	1,800,000
Fall in investment value (non-adjusting event)	0
Write down of receivable	(116,000)
Inventory write down (161 – 141)	(20,000)
Seizure of assets (non-adjusting event)	0
	1,664,000

5.20   The correct answer is: On 1 October 20X8, GD made a rights issue of 1 new share for every 3 shares held at a price of $175. The market price on that date was $200.

An adjusting event is an event that provides further evidence of a condition that already existed at the reporting date.

A non-adjusting event relates to the situation where the condition did not exist at the reporting date.

6   Presentation of published financial statements

6.1   The correct answer is: Finance costs.

Finance costs must be included on the face of the statement of profit or loss.

6.2   The correct answer is:

- Revenue $1,260,000
- Current assets $361,000

The amounts are calculated as:

	$
Revenue – per trial balance	1,275,000
Less deposit on goods not yet despatched	(15,000)
	1,260,000
Current assets	
Inventory – per trial balance	186,000
Receivables – per trial balance	175,000
	361,000

Note. Cash and cash equivalents are a credit balance, indicating an overdrawn (liability) position.

6.3   The correct answer is: It includes other comprehensive income.

Other comprehensive income is included within the aggregated amount for total comprehensive income.

The statement of changes in equity is a primary statement and includes gains taken directly to reserves.

It is presented with the same prominence as the statement of profit or loss and statement of financial position. All gains are included whether they are reported in the statement of profit or loss or in reserves.

6.4   The correct answer is:

- Revenue $3,335,000
- Administrative expenses $539,000

Revenue:

The revenue figure is not impacted by the irrecoverable debt and so the figure for revenue is unchanged from the trial balance extract.

Administrative expenses:

	$
Per trial balance	455,000
Buildings depreciation	48,000
Irrecoverable debt expense	36,000
	539,000

The trial balance extract shows 'land and buildings' at a cost of $2,500,000. The cost of land included in this is $900,000 and therefore the cost of the buildings must be $1,600,000 ($2,500,000 – $900,000).

Land is not depreciated; however, the buildings are depreciated at 3% on a straight-line basis.

Therefore, the buildings depreciation is $1,600,000 × 0.03 = $48,000.

The irrecoverable debt of $36,000 must be written off to the statement of profit or loss, and will therefore increase the administrative expenses.

6.5   The correct answer is: $185,000.

	$'000
Profit for the year (after tax, before dividends) (W)	110
Unrealised revaluation gain (150 – 75)	75
Total comprehensive income	185

Working: Profit for the year	
Retained earnings (400 – 340)	60
Add back dividends	50
Profit for year after taxation	110

6.6   The correct answer is: $629,000.

The amounts are calculated as:

	$
Cost of sales – per trial balance	554,000
Depreciation of plant and equipment:	
P&E with a revised useful life (120 – [120 × 12.5% × 4 years]) = 60/2 years	30,000
Other P&E (480 – 120) × 12.5%	45,000
	629,000

6.7   The correct answer is: Loss on closure of bottling division.

This must be disclosed on the face of the statement of profit or loss per IFRS 5.

IAS 1 requires disclosure of items which are of such size, nature or importance that disclosure is necessary to explain performance of entity. However, such disclosure may be in the notes, and does not have to be on the face of the statement of profit or loss.

6.8   The correct answer is:

	DR $	CR $
Receivables	3,000	
Plant and equipment – accumulated depreciation	41,000	
Loss on disposal of non-current assets	2,000	
Plant and equipment – cost		46,000

The obsolete plant and equipment has been sold, and must therefore be removed from Leapfrog Co's non-current assets.

The cost to be removed (credited) is $46,000.

The accumulated depreciation to be removed (debited) must be $41,000, since the carrying amount was $5,000.

The proceeds from the sale are $3,000, but this has not yet been received so the receivables should be increased (debited) by $3,000.

Given that the sales proceeds are $3,000 and the asset has a carrying amount of $5,000 there is a loss on disposal of $2,000, which will be an expense (debit) in the statement of profit or loss.

6.9   The correct answer is: An upward revaluation of the company's assets.

It is the only one of the four options that is a gain or loss accounted for as other comprehensive income.

6.10   The correct answer is:

- Administrative expenses $201,000
- Finance costs $14,000

The amounts are calculated as:

	$
Administrative expenses – per trial balance	180,000
Building depreciation ([960 – 260] × 3%)	21,000
	201,000
Finance costs – per trial balance	7,000
Interest accrual ([280 × 5%] – 7)	7,000
	14,000

6.11   The correct answer is: $92,000 gain.

The write down would be treated as an expense in profit or loss because the asset was previously held at historic cost; the upwards revaluation is recorded as other comprehensive income.

6.12   The correct answer is: $1,480,000.

	$
Inventory at 1 January 20X4 per TB extract	420,000
Inventory purchases per TB extract	1,425,000
Closing inventory (per additional note (2))	(562,000)
Loss on disposal of non-current assets (per additional note (1))	2,000
Plant and equipment depreciation (W)	195,000
	1,480,000

Working: Plant and equipment depreciation

	$
Plant and equipment – cost at 1 January 20X4 per TB extract	1,055,000
Plant and equipment – accumulated depreciation at 1 January 20X4 per TB extract	(400,000)
Less carrying amount of obsolete plant and equipment	(5,000)
	650,000
Depreciation charge ($650,000 × 30%)	195,000

Always assume a full year of depreciation in the year of acquisition and none in the year of disposal, unless the question states otherwise.

6.13 The correct answer is: $36 million.

	$m
Profit for the year	29
Revaluations (14 – 7)	7
	36

6.14 The correct answers are:

- Tax expense $62,000
- Current tax payable $52,000
- Share capital $560,000
- Share premium $120,000

The amounts are calculated as follows:

	$
Tax expense	
Charge for the year (per note (b))	52,000
Add underprovision relating to prior year	10,000
	62,000
Current tax payable (per note (b))	52,000
Share capital – per trial balance	560,000
Share premium – per trial balance	120,000

6.15 The correct answer is:

	Share capital $	Share premium $	Retained earnings $	Total $
Balance brought forward at 1 January 20X4	1,450,000	240,000	370,000	2,060,000
Share issue	50,000	10,000		60,000
Dividend paid			(360,000)	(360,000)
Profit for the period				
Balance carried forward at 1 January 20X4	1,500,000	250,000		

7 Statements of cash flows

7.1 The correct answer is: Repayment of an overdraft.

An overdraft is a borrowing facility repayable on demand. The repayment of an overdraft will increase the amount of cash which is the bottom line of the statement of cash flows and will be included in the increase or decrease in cash and cash equivalents for the year.

The issue of ordinary shares would be a cash inflow under 'financing'.

The repurchase of a long-term loan means the company is paying the loan back and this would be a cash outflow under 'financing'.

Dividends paid can be shown as an outflow in either the operating activities section or in the financing outflow section of the statement of cash flows.

7.2 The correct answer is: The statement of profit or loss charge for taxation for the current year.

The profit or loss charge is not shown in the statement of cash flows; rather, the statement of cash flows will show the actual tax paid.

7.3 The correct answer is: Entirely excluded.

Revaluations have no cash flow implications.

7.4 The correct answer is: The statement of profit or loss charge for depreciation for the year.

Depreciation is a non-cash item and so does not appear as a cash outflow. It is added back to the profit before tax figure as a non-cash item when preparing the statement of cash flows under the indirect method.

7.5 The correct answer is: $520,000.

	$
Share capital increase (1,600,000 – 1,200,000)	400,000
Share premium increase (400,000 – 280,000)	120,000
Total	520,000

7.6 The correct answer is: $204,000.

NON-CURRENT ASSET COSTS

	$		$
Opening balance	1,096,000	Disposal	150,000
Revaluation (240 – 140)	100,000		
Cash paid (balancing figure)	204,000	Closing balance	1,250,000
	1,400,000		1,400,000

7.7 The correct answer is: Gain on sale of a motor vehicle.

The gain on sale of the motor vehicle is a non-cash item which has increased profit before tax. It should be deducted from the profit before tax figure when arriving at net cash flow from operating activities.

The surplus on the revaluation of property is also a non-cash item. This does not however impact the profit before tax and so is excluded from the statement of cash flows.

7.8 The correct answers are:

- Bank current account in domestic currency.
- Bank overdraft.
- Petty cash float.
- Bank current account in foreign currency.

The short-term deposit is not included in cash. It could potentially have been included as a cash equivalent, but for this to be the case it would need to be repayable on demand. This is only the case if it can be withdrawn without notice (in practice within 24 hours) but the deposit in question has a three-month notice period.

Therefore it is neither cash nor a cash equivalent.

7.9 The correct answer is: $180,000.

NON-CURRENT ASSETS – COST

	$		$
B/d	180,000	Disposals	80,000
Therefore purchases	140,000	C/d	240,000
	320,000		320,000

DEPRECIATION

	$		$
		B/d	120,000
Disposals	50,000	Charge for the year	70,000
C/d	140,000		
	190,000		190,000

DISPOSALS

	$		$
Cost	80,000	Accumulated depreciation	50,000
		Proceeds	20,000
		Therefore loss	10,000
	80,000		80,000

	$
Cash from operations	300,000
Cash inflow:	
Disposal proceeds	20,000
	320,000
Cash outflow:	
Purchases of non-current assets	(140,000)
Therefore net cash increase	180,000

Note. Adjustments for depreciation and loss on disposal will already be included in final figure for net cash flow from operating activities.

7.10   The correct answer is: $38,000.

Working: Interest payable

	$
Balance b/d	12,000
Finance charge per SPLOCI	41,000
	53,000
Cash paid (balancing figure)	(38,000)
Balance c/d	15,000

Working: Interest payable (alternative)

INTEREST PAYABLE

	$		$
Cash paid (bal. figure)	38,000	Balance c/d	12,000
Balance c/d	15,000		41,000
	53,000		53,000

7.11   The correct answers are:

- Cash at a bank

- Bank overdraft

- Current asset investments readily convertible into known amounts of cash and which can be sold without disrupting the company's business

Cash at a bank and a bank overdraft would be deemed to be cash whereas current asset investments readily convertible into known amounts of cash would be considered to be cash equivalents.

Equity investments and long-term loans do not generally fulfil the description of cash equivalents.

7.12   The correct answers are:

- Proposed dividends
- Bonus issue of shares
- Surplus on revaluation of a non-current asset

Proposed dividends, a bonus issue of shares and the revaluation of a non-current asset are all non-cash transactions and so would not appear in the statement of cash flows.

7.13   The correct answer is: Profit on sale of non-current asset.

When a non-current asset is disposed of at a profit, the profit (or gain) increases the profit before tax figure. This is a non-cash item and so must be deducted when deriving the figure for cash from operating activities.

The amortisation charge for the year is a non-cash item which reduces the profit before tax figure and so this is added back. The surplus on the revaluation of property is also a non-cash item. This does not, however, impact the profit before tax and so is excluded from the statement of cash flows. A loan repayment is shown as a cash outflow in the financing section of the statement of cash flows.

7.14   The correct answer is: Cash flows from operating activities reconciliation: $(9,000); Cash inflow: $30,000

The $9,000 profit is shown before profit before tax in the statement of profit or loss. As it is not a cash flow, it is deducted from the profit before tax figure in the reconciliation of profit before tax to net cash from operating activities.

The cash received was $30,000 and this is an inflow under the heading of cash flows from investing activities.

7.15   The correct answer is: It will be shown as a cash outflow under financing activities.

The capital element of the lease payments is shown within cash flows from financing activities, whereas the interest elements of the lease payments are accounted for as a finance cost and will be deducted in arriving at cash flows from operating activities.

8   General principles of taxation

8.1   The correct answer is: Tax evasion is the illegal manipulation of the tax system to avoid paying taxes due. Tax avoidance is tax planning – legally arranging affairs so as to minimise the tax liability.

Tax evasion is a way of paying less tax by illegal methods whereas tax avoidance is a way of arranging your affairs to take advantage of the tax rules to pay as little tax as possible. This is legal.

8.2   The correct answer is: The difference between the total amount of tax due to be paid and the amount actually collected by the tax authority.

The tax gap is the gap between the tax theoretically collectable and the amount actually collected.

8.3   The correct answer is: It should raise as much money as possible for the government.

A 'good tax' should be convenient, equitable, certain and efficient.

8.4   The correct answer is: Power of arrest.

Tax authorities have the power to:
*   Review and query returns submitted to them
*   Request special reports or returns
*   Examine records which support the returns which have been made
*   Enter and search a business

8.5   The correct answer is: To ensure tax is paid early.

Setting deadlines is unlikely to result in the early payment of taxes; however, it will allow taxpayers to know the date by which they need to have paid their taxes. Tax authorities are able to forecast the timing of tax receipts and give a point of reference after which penalties can be levied.

8.6   The correct answer is: The process of earmarking tax revenues for specific types of expenditure.

Hypothecation is also known as 'ring fencing' and describes the situation where revenues raised from tax are used to finance specific types of expenditure. For example, in the UK, motorists in inner London are charged a 'congestion charge' and revenues raised can only be spent on London transport.

8.7   The correct answer is: Effective incidence.

Effective incidence describes the individual or entity that bears the end cost of a tax, whereas formal incidence describes the individual or entity that has direct contact with the tax authorities.

8.8   The correct answer is: The amount of tax due to be paid and the amount actually collected.

Tax authorities always aim to minimise the tax gap.

8.9   The correct answer is: A progressive tax.

A progressive tax structure exists where an increasing proportion of income is taken in tax as income rises. Here BM pays tax at a rate of 10% on taxable profits of $30,000 whilst BV pays tax at 12.5% on taxable profits of $60,000.

8.10   The correct answers are:

- Imprecise and vague tax laws
- Very high tax rates

Imprecise and vague tax laws mean that individuals or companies may consider it easier to try to find tax loopholes, and therefore the incidence of tax evasion and avoidance may increase.

High tax rates mean high tax bills for individuals and companies, and therefore may increase the incentive to avoid or evade paying tax in order to reduce costs.

8.11   The correct answer is: Formal incidence.

Formal incidence describes the individual or entity that has direct contact with the tax authorities whereas effective incidence describes the individual or entity that bears the end cost of a tax. Here the effective incidence is on B's customers.

8.12   The correct answer is: The person or entity that finally bears the cost of the tax.

Formal incidence describes the individual or entity that has direct contact with the tax authorities whereas the effective incidence describes the individual or entity that bears the end cost of a tax.

8.13   The correct answer is: Power to detain company officials.

Tax authorities have the power to:

- Review and query returns submitted to them
- Request special reports or returns
- Examine records which support the returns that have been made
- Enter and search a business

8.14   The correct answer is: The tax authority whose tax laws apply to an entity.

Tax jurisdiction refers to the power of a tax authority to charge and collect tax. The competent jurisdiction is the country whose tax laws apply to the entity.

8.15   The correct answer is:

	Tax avoidance	Tax evasion	Tax gap
The use of legitimate tax rules to minimise the amount of tax payable	☑		
The difference between the tax theoretically collectable and the amount actually collected			☑
Seeking to pay too little tax by deliberately misleading the tax authorities		☑	

9 Direct taxation

9.1 The correct answer is: $12,000.

	$	$
Sale:		450,000
Selling price		(15,000)
Charges		435,000
Less purchase:		
Cost	375,000	
Fees	12,000	
		387,000
Profit		48,000
Tax ($48,000 × 25%)		12,000

9.2 The correct answer is: It benefits the taxpayer as it reduces the tax payable.

The tax payable is the same regardless of whether it is collected by PAYE or in one lump sum.

9.3 The correct answers are:

- Individual income tax, usually deducted at source
- Corporate income tax

Direct taxes are imposed on the income of individuals and the profits made by companies. Import duties and sales tax are examples of indirect taxes.

9.4 The correct answer is: $23,000.

	$
Profit for the year (excluding depreciation)	128,000
Tax depreciation ($72,000 × 50%)	(36,000)
Taxable profit	92,000
Tax at 25%	23,000

9.5 The correct answer is: Pay $40,000 tax for the year and have no loss to carry forward.

The entity's taxable profits of $480,000 would be reduced by the $320,000 tax losses brought forward. The entity would then have a taxable profit of $160,000 on which tax of $40,000 (25%) would be due. All of the tax losses brought forward would have been used and there would be no loss to carry forward.

9.6 The correct answer is: $22,250.

This is calculated as follows:

	$
Accounting profit	72,000
Add disallowable expenditure:	
Entertaining	15,000
Accounting depreciation	12,000
	99,000
Less tax depreciation (40,000 × 25%)	(10,000)
	89,000
Tax (25% × $89,000)	22,250

9.7 The correct answer is: Capital gains tax.

Direct taxes relate to taxes charged on income or profits, such as capital gains tax. Sales tax, excise duties and property tax all relate to taxes on spending and are examples of an indirect tax.

9.8 The correct answer is: Payment of tax on a capital gain can be delayed if the full proceeds from the sale of an asset are reinvested in a replacement asset.

9.9 The correct answer is: $10,000.

Tax payable by shareholders:

	$
Dividend received	150,000
Tax credit (150,000/75 × 25)	50,000
Gross dividend	200,000
Tax at 30%	60,000
Less tax credit	(50,000)
Tax to pay	10,000

9.10 The correct answer is: A classical system.

Here the entity and the shareholder have been treated completely separately for the purpose of calculating tax. This is the classical system.

9.11 The correct answer is: $121,750.

	$
Accounting profit	500,000
Entertaining expenses	51,000
Political donation	36,000
Non-taxable income	(100,000)
Taxable profit	487,000
Tax at 25%	121,750

9.12   The correct answers are:

- It enables tax to be saved at the highest marginal rate.

- It improves the cash flow of the group by enabling the trading loss to be used as soon as possible.

9.13   The correct answer is: $15,000.

This is calculated as follows:

	$
Purchase price of asset	420,000
Add import duties	30,000
	450,000
Indexation allowance (450,000 × 40%)	180,000
	630,000
Selling price less selling costs (700,000 – 10,000)	(690,000)
Capital gain on disposal	60,000
Tax payable ($60,000 × 25%)	15,000

9.14   The correct answer is: For the year ended 31 December 20X2 there is a balancing **charge** of **$850**.

The entity has received tax depreciation of $3,750 on the asset ([$6,000 × 50%] + [$6,000 – $3,000] × 25%). However, the asset has only fallen in value by $2,900 ($6,000 – $3,100).

Therefore on disposal there will be a balancing charge of $850 ($3,750 – $2,900).

9.15   The correct answer is: $281,000.

	$	$
Profit before tax		300,000
Add: depreciation	30,000	
disallowed expenses	25,000	
		55,000
		355,000
Less: non-taxable income	50,000	
tax depreciation	24,000	
		74,000
Taxable profit		281,000

10 International and indirect taxation

10.1 The correct answer is: Tax deducted at source before payment of interest or dividends.

Withholding tax is a tax which is deducted and paid to the local tax authority before funds (such as dividends and royalties) can be remitted overseas.

10.2 The correct answer is: To mitigate taxing overseas income twice.

Double taxable treaties deal with overseas income.

10.3 The correct answer is: Specific unit tax.

This is a specific unit tax as it is a charge on each unit (litre) of a specific product (imported petroleum products).

The answer cannot be a general consumption tax because the tax applies to a particular product only, and is therefore not 'general'.

Ad valorem taxes are based on the value of the items; for example, sales tax (VAT).

10.4 The correct answers are:

- Indirect tax
- Formal incidence

Sales tax is an indirect tax as it is a tax on expenditure (or 'consumption'). The entity has direct contact with the tax authorities and so the formal incidence is on the entity.

10.5 The correct answer is: $50,000.

	$
Sales excluding sales tax ($138,000 × 100/115)	120,000
Cost of goods	(70,000)
Profit	50,000

10.6 The correct answer is: An individual who purchases goods in a shop – the price includes sales tax.

Sales tax is an indirect tax because it relates to consumption/spending. Sales tax is collected by the shop and passed on to the tax authorities via its sales tax return.

Corporate income tax, employee tax and capital gain tax are all direct taxes as they relate to income/profits.

10.7 The correct answer is: Sales tax.

Sales tax is an indirect tax because it relates to consumption/spending. Withholding tax, employee tax and corporate income tax are all direct taxes as they relate to income/profits.

10.8 The correct answer is: The end consumer.

Provided that the supplier of raw materials, the retailer and the wholesaler are registered for sales tax, they merely act as tax collectors – it is the end consumer who suffers the tax.

10.9 The correct answer is: Place of effective management.

In the event that an entity is resident in more than one country, the OECD Model Tax Convention states that the entity will be deemed to be resident only in the country of its effective management.

10.10 The correct answer is: $30,000.

Tax due in Country Y:

	$
Gross dividend	100,000
Add underlying tax	20,000
	120,000
Tax @ 40%	48,000
Less double tax relief for WHT- withholding tax	(10,000)
double tax relief for ULT - underlying tax	(20,000)
Tax payable	18,000

Double tax relief = 10,000 + 20,000 = $30,000

10.11 The correct answer is: Corporate income tax is paid on profits remitted by the branch.

Corporate income tax is due on all profits of the branch, not just those remitted.

10.12 The correct answer is: $5,550.

This is calculated as:

	$
Cost	14,000
Excise duty	3,000
	17,000
Sales tax @ 15%	2,550
	19,550

Taxes paid = $3,000 + $2,550 = $5,550

10.13 The correct answer is: $0.

Tax paid in Country A:

WHT: 12,000
ULT: $40,000

Tax due in Country B:

	$
Gross dividend	80,000
Add underlying tax	40,000
	120,000
Tax @ 30%	36,000
Less DTR for WHT	(12,000)
DTR for ULT (capped at $24,000)	(24,000)
Tax payable	0*

*Tax credit cannot create a refund of tax

10.14 The correct answer is: $28,500.

Input tax attributable to exempt outputs cannot be reclaimed. Input tax attributable to zero-rate outputs can be reclaimed, because these outputs are considered to be taxable, but at the zero rate.

10.15 The correct answer is: $12,000.

	$
Output tax 264,500 × 15/115	34,500
Input tax (170,000 − 20,000) × 15%	(22,500)
Tax payable	12,000

11 Working capital and the operating cycle

11.1 The correct answer is: An aggressive policy.

Three possible policies exist to finance working capital.

- Conservative policy – all of the permanent assets (current and non-current) and some of the fluctuating current assets are financed by long-term funding.

- Aggressive policy – all of the fluctuating and part of the permanent current assets are financed by short-term funding.

- Moderate policy – short-term funding is used to finance the fluctuating current assets, and the permanent assets (current and non-current) are financed by long-term funding.

11.2 The correct answer is: Increasing levels of long-term borrowings.

CIMA defines overtrading as 'where an entity enters into trading commitments in excess of its available short-term resources'.

CIMA Official Terminology 2005

Even if an overtrading business operates at a profit, the lack of working capital may mean that they lack the cash to pay debts as they fall due - this can lead to apparently profitable businesses going into liquidation.

11.3 The correct answer is: 108 days.

This is calculated as: 46 days + 43 days − 67 days + 32 days + 54 days = 108 days.

11.4 The correct answer is: A dramatic reduction in sales revenue.

A company that overtrades is doing too much too quickly.

11.5 The correct answers are:

- Shareholders will not be happy as resources could be used elsewhere to generate a return.

- The entity has invested too much in receivables, inventory and cash and holds few payables.

- The entity has an excess of working capital.

11.6 The correct answer is: Short-term financing of $1 million; permanent financing of $14 million.

Short-term finance is matched to fluctuating current assets.

A policy where short-term financing is $0.5 million and permanent financing is $14.5 million is a conservative policy.

Short-term financing of $2 million and permanent financing of $13 million, and short-term financing of $4 million and permanent financing of $11 million are both are aggressive policies.

11.7 The correct answer is: 114 days.

Inventory days	– (8 ÷ ($48m × 60%))	× 365 days	= 101.4 days
Receivable days	= ($10/$48)	× 365 days	= 76 days
Payable days	= (5 ÷ ($48 × 60%))	× 365 days	= 63.4 days
Cash operating cycle = 101.4 days		+ 76 days – 63.4 days	= 114 days

11.8 The correct answer is: $6.750 million.

	$m
Inventory ($30m × 0.7 × 2.5/12)	4.375
Accounts receivable ($30m × 2/12)	5.000
Accounts payable ($30m × 0.7 × 1.5/12)	(2.625)
	6.750

11.9 The correct answer is: 115 days.

Inventory turnover period = 102 – 54 + 67 = 115 days

11.10 The correct answers are:

Inventory days	44.6
Trade receivables days	57.8

Inventory days	= (inventory/COS) × 365 days	= (220/1,800) × 365 days	= 44.6 days
Trade receivable days	= (average trade receivables/credit sales for the year) × 365 days	= (350/2,600 × 0.85) × 365 days	= 57.8 days

11.11 The correct answer is: Inventory days plus accounts receivable days less accounts payable days.

11.12 The correct answers are:

Trade receivables days	24.9
Payables days	64.2

Receivable days = (average trade receivables/credit sales for the year) × 365 days = ([(800 + 840)/2]/12,000) × 365 days = 24.9 days

Payable days = (average trade payables/purchases on credit for the year) × 365 days = ([(1,120 + 1,160)/2]/[6,400 + 1,200 – 1,120]) × 365 = 64.2 days

Purchases on credit for the year are calculated by taking the 20X1 cost of sales and adding the 20X1 inventories and subtracting the 20X0 inventories.

11.13 The correct answer is: Sale of a non-current asset on credit at its carrying amount.

The receipt of the full amount of cash from a trade receivable will increase cash and reduce receivables by the same amount.

The payment of an account payable will reduce cash and reduce payables by the same amount.

The purchase of inventory on credit would increase inventory and increase payables by the same amount.

Hence all of these will have no impact on the amount of working capital.

11.14 The correct answer is: 36.5 days.

Current ratio = current assets/current liabilities = 2

Here = ($3m + inventory)/$2m = 2

So inventory = $1m

If cost of sales is $10m then inventory days = $(1/10) \times 365 = 36.5$ days

11.15 The correct answer is:

	True	False
Working capital should increase as sales increase.	Y	
An increase in the working capital/cash operating cycle will decrease profitability.	Y	
Overtrading is also known as undercapitalisation.	Y	

Statement 1 is correct. If a business is profitable then an increase in sales should translate to more working capital.

Statement 2 is correct. The greater the cash operating cycle, the greater the working capital investment need is. Greater working capital means more cash tied up which is therefore not earning profit.

Statement 3 is correct. Overtrading (or undercapitalisation) is where a business is over-reliant on short-term finance to support its operations. It is trying to do too much too quickly with little long-term capital.

12 Receivables, payables and inventory

12.1 The correct answer is: Deciding what credit limits customers should be given.

12.2 The correct answer is: Negotiation of the price of the goods.

The credit cycle begins with the receipt of the customer's order. Price negotiations take place prior to this point.

12.3 The correct answer is: Selling invoices to a finance company for less than their face value while continuing to collect the cash from the customer.

Here the entity maintains the administration of the sales ledger but sells selected invoices to the invoice discounter purely to obtain an advance of cash.

12.4 The correct answer is: The borrowing is repayable over a number of years.

Factoring is a short-term method of raising finance.

12.5 The correct answers are:

- Difficulty in obtaining credit from new suppliers
- Reduction in credit rating

12.6 The correct answer is: $7 decrease.

Cash flow if debts are factored:

	$
90% of $90 received	81

Current cash flow:

40% of $100 paid in 30 days	40
60% × 80% of $100 received later	48
	88

Difference = $7

12.7 The correct answer is: The factoring company purchases a selection of invoices at a discount, thus providing the client with a source of short-term finance.

True invoice discounting is a one-off arrangement made purely for the advance of cash to the client to cover a short-term cash shortfall.

While a factoring company may take over sales invoicing, this is an administrative service and has no financial component. It therefore has nothing to do with invoice discounting.

Enforcing correct administration is an administrative function that will be carried out by the factoring company if it is responsible for debt collection. It has nothing to do with the provision of finance.

Advancing finance to the client is effectively 'factor finance', or the provision of short-term finance against the total receivables ledger rather than against individual invoices.

12.8 The correct answers are:

- Provision of finance against the client's outstanding receivables
- Protection against irrecoverable debts
- Administration of the client's invoicing and debt collection

The factor is concerned with the receivables ledger department (not payables ledger) and can be involved in its administration.

Protection against irrecoverable debts is provided if factoring is without recourse, and finance may be provided by making payments to the client before the debts are collected.

Credit rating information will normally be provided by a credit rating agency.

12.9 The correct answer is: 44.9%

Payment will be made 30 days early.

$$\text{Number of compounding periods} = \frac{365}{30} = 12.167$$

$$1 + r = \left(\frac{1.00}{0.97}\right)^{12.167}$$

$$= 1.4486$$

$$\therefore r = 44.86\% \text{ or } 44.9\% \text{ to one decimal place}$$

12.10   The correct answer is: $25,000.

(Total sales × 2%) + $5,000. 'Without recourse' means that the factor carries the risk of the irrecoverable debts.

12.11   The correct answer is: Saving of $46,000.

A saving of $36,000 ignores the effect of the changes on the level of inventories and payables.

Increases of $46,000 and $36,000 are wrong because they assume that the financing cost will increase not decrease.

Current level of receivables	= $2m × (90/365)	= $493,151
New level of receivables	= $2m × 80% × (30/365)	= $131,507
Current financing requirement	= $500,000 + $493,150 − $30,000	= $963,150
New financing requirement	= $400,000 + $131,507 − $24,000	= $507,507
Reduction in financing requirement	= $963,150 − $507,507	= $455,643
Reduction in financing cost	= $455,643 × 10%	= $45,564
		(round to $46,000).

12.12   The correct answer is: $28,800.

Factor advances 80% of $2,190,000 = $1,752,000

Trade receivables	= 50/365 × $1,752,000	= $240,000
Interest at 12%	= $240,000 × 12%	= $28,800

12.13   The correct answer is: 78 days.

$8,000 + purchases − $12,000 = COS = $103,628

Balancing figure for credit purchases is 107,628.

Using the trade payable days formula: (23,000/107,628) × 365 days = 78 days.

12.14   The correct answers are:

- X Co will be dissatisfied with what NC owes it.
- Overall NC is very good at paying suppliers within due dates.

12.15   The correct answer is: Loss of goodwill as a result of being unable to complete customer orders due to lack of inventory.

Insurance, storage and loss of interest are all costs of holding inventory. If inventory is held then customer orders will be complete and so no goodwill will be lost.

12.16   The correct answer is: The cost of holding one unit of inventory for one year.

D is the annual demand.

Co is the cost of ordering.

12.17 The correct answer is: 8,000 units.

The cost of holding one item in inventory for a year is $4. Note that this is also subject to the discounts.

The EOQ without the discounts is 800, but this is not the most economic order quantity when the discounts are taken into account.

Quantity	800	1,000	4,000	8,000
No. of orders	25	20	5	3
Order	$1,600	$1,280	$320	$192
Holding*	$1,600	$1,980	$7,840	$15,520
Purchase	$800,000	$792,000	$784,000	$776,000
Cost	$803,200	$795,260	$792,160	$791,712

*Remember that holding cost = (order quantity × cost of holding one unit for a year)/2 and don't forget to take account of the discount as well.

Therefore 8,000 units give the lowest cost.

If the company places orders of 8,000 units, three orders will need to be made to meet the 20,000 unit requirement.

12.18 The correct answer is: 1 only.

The EOQ model finds order quantity only.

The re-order levels are normally set by reference to lead time and demand in lead time. Buffer inventory is decided by management.

12.19 The correct answer is: 2,208 units.

$$EOQ = \sqrt{\frac{2C_oD}{C_h}}$$

$$= \sqrt{\frac{2 \times \$100 \times 39,000}{\$1.60}}$$

= 2,208 units

12.20 The correct answer is: 1,500 units.

The annual demand of 39,000 boxes is spread evenly over the year. Weekly demand is therefore 39,000/52 = 750 boxes per week.

It takes two weeks for an order to be delivered to JD's premises so JD needs to have 2 weeks × 750 = 1,500 boxes to make sure it never runs out of inventory.

13 Managing cash

13.1 The correct answer is: Expected gain on the disposal of a piece of land.

When preparing a cash forecast only **cash** is considered. Here the question talks about a **gain** on disposal and gains are not cash. Gains are where the cash received is greater than the carrying amount of the asset.

13.2   The correct answer is: $5,500,000.

	$
Opening receivables cash received during year	460,000
Cash received ($5,400,000 × 20%)	1,080,000
11 months of credit sales ([$5,400,000 × 80%] × 11/12)	3,960,000
	5,500,000

13.3   The correct answer is: Depreciation of the new rolling mill.

Depreciation is a non-cash item and should therefore be excluded from a cash flow forecast.

13.4   The correct answer is: $1,495,425.

$242,000 + $1,500,000 − ($1,500,000 × 60/365) = $1,495,425

13.5   The correct answer is: $273,510.

Receivables at 31 March 20X7 = $290,510/365 days × 49 days = $39,000

Cash received is therefore:

	$
Opening receivables	22,000
Credit sales	290,510
Closing receivables	(39,000)
Cash received	273,510

13.6   The correct answer is: $395,000.

This is calculated as:

	$
Inventory b/f	39,000
Inventory purchased (balancing figure)	384,000
Inventory c/f	(51,000)
Inventory used	372,000
Payables b/f	58,000
Purchases (from inventory working)	384,000
Payables c/f	(47,000)
Cash paid	395,000

13.7 The correct answer is: $45,833.

Gross profit margin is 50%, therefore cost of sales are 50% of the sales price

Annual cost of sales = 50% × $1.1 million = $550,000

As inventories remain constant, this is also the annual purchase cost, which is spread evenly over the year.

Thus one month's purchases = $550,000/12 = $45,833

This is the value of one month's extra trade credit, ie the cash benefit to be derived from delaying payment by one month.

13.8 The correct answer is: $3,239.

January sales amount to $12,500 and sales during February to December will be $3,409 per month ([$50,000 × 75%]/11).

Therefore in March cash received will be 40% of February's sales plus 55% of March's sales = $3,239.

13.9 The correct answer is: $35,100.

April: Sales = $40,000; therefore cost of sales = $30,000 and closing payables = $4,500

May: Sales = $48,000; therefore cost of sales = $36,000 and closing payables = $5,400

PAYABLES ACCOUNT (MAY)

	$		$
Cash (bal. figure)	35,100	Opening balance	4,500
Closing	5,400	Cost of sales	36,000
	40,500		40,500

13.10 The correct answer is: Compared with other types of loan it is quick and easy to set up.

Interest is only paid on the amount borrowed, not the full facility.

13.11 The correct answer is: Trade receivable factoring.

13.12 The correct answer is: Treasury bills.

Treasury bills are a form of cash investment.

13.13 The correct answer is: The terms of an overdraft are more easily changed to accommodate different needs within the entity.

13.14 The correct answer is: Advances against collections.

The question asked which of the methods would **not** reduce the risks of irrecoverable debts when trading overseas. Export factoring, forfaiting and documentary credits are all methods of insuring against irrecoverable debts risk from overseas receivables.

An advance against collections from a factor or a discount house can reduce the amount of funds an entity has invested in foreign receivables, but it does not reduce the risk of irrecoverable debts.

13.15 The correct answer is: Credit insurance.

Credit insurance is an insurance which can be taken out (at a cost to the entity) which the entity can claim on in the event that an overseas receivable fails to pay the amounts owed.

Credit insurance is therefore not a source of finance.

13.16 The correct answer is: Both statements are true.

It is important not to confuse the coupon rate and the yield to maturity, especially when calculating the selling price of a bond.

13.17   The correct answer is: Investment in equities.

Short-term cash surpluses will not normally be invested in equities owing to the risks associated with achieving a return over a short period.

13.18   The correct answer is: It is a method of providing medium-term export finance.

13.19   The correct answer is: Certificates of deposit are non-negotiable.

13.20   The correct answer is: A document issued by a bank on behalf of a customer authorising a person to draw money to a specified amount from its branches or correspondents, usually in another country, when the conditions set out in the document have been met.

Letters of credit provide a method of payment in international trade which gives the exporter a risk free method of obtaining credit.

Practice mock questions

Questions

1 Which TWO of the following statements/provisions are NOT specific requirements of the Sarbanes-Oxley Act 2002?

☐ Auditors are expressly forbidden from carrying out most non-audit services.

☐ The establishment of the Public Company Accounting Oversight Board

☑ Annual reports should state whether a company has complied with the provisions of the Act and if they haven't, provide an explanation.

☑ All members of audit committees should be independent and at least two members should be financial experts.

☐ The chief executive officer should certify the appropriateness of a company's financial statements.

2 Under the current structure of regulatory bodies, which organisation is responsible for seeking out the views of its members and passing them on in summary form to the International Accounting Standards Board (IASB)?

○ IFRS Interpretations Committee

○ International Organization of Securities Commissions

○ IFRS Foundation

○ IFRS Advisory Council

3 Which ONE of the following is NOT a recommendation of the UK Corporate Governance Code for improving the effectiveness of the board?

○ All directors should be able to allocate sufficient time to the company to discharge their responsibilities effectively.

○ There should be a formal, rigorous and transparent procedure for the appointment of new directors to the board.

○ The board should be supplied in a timely manner with information in a form and of a quality appropriate to enable it to discharge its duties.

○ The board should undertake a formal and rigorous evaluation of its own performance and that of its committees and individual directors at least every five years.

4 Which ONE of the following does NOT describe a process by which a country may adopt International Financial Reporting Standards?

○ Adoption as local accounting standards with few or no amendments for their particular countries

○ Persuasive influence in formulating local accounting standards, gradually 'narrowing the gap' between local standards and IFRS Standards

○ Model for local accounting standards, adopting IFRS Standards, but adapting them to suit local needs

○ Work with the IASB to develop a common conceptual framework in the long term to ensure future convergence of international standards

5 Which ONE of the following best describes one of the roles of the IFRS Foundation?

○ It prepares and publishes exposure drafts.

○ It provides the International Accounting Standards Board with views of its members relating to current discussion documents.

◉ It promotes the International Accounting Standards Board, its work and the use of IFRS.

○ It clarifies issues where conflicting interpretations have developed. ✓

6 As an accountant in business, Priti has been asked by her colleagues to manipulate the results of the quarterly management accounts to ensure that she and the team will be entitled to a large bonus.

From the list below select which threat is represented, and which ethical principle is being threatened.

☐ Confidentiality

☑ Integrity

☐ Intimidation

☐ Objectivity ✓

☑ Self-interest

☐ Self-review

7 The IASB's *Conceptual Framework for Financial Reporting* identifies two fundamental and four enhancing qualitative characteristics of financial statements.

Choose the correct options from the picklist below to show the fundamental and enhancing qualitative characteristics.

Fundamental qualitative characteristics	Enhancing qualitative characteristics
Rel ▼	Com. ▼
F ▼	Und ▼
	Ver ▼
	Timelin ▼

Picklist:

Accruals
Comparability
Consistency
Disclosure
Faithful representation
Materiality
Relevance
Reliability
Timeliness
Understandability
Verifiability

✓

8   Which of the following definitions represents current cost?

○   The net amount of cash expected to be received from selling an asset

○   The amount of cash that would need to be paid in order to acquire a new asset today

○   The amount of cash in today's money that would need to be paid to acquire an asset in 20 years' time

⊘   The amount of cash that would need to be paid in order to acquire an equivalent asset today

9   Which measurement basis from the IASB's *Conceptual Framework for Financial Reporting* is defined in the following statement?

'The cost of an equivalent asset at the measurement date.'

○   Historical cost

○   Fair value

○   Value in use

⊘   Current cost

10   The following information is an extract from the trial balance for XCB Co at 31 March 20X4:

	$	$
Purchases	6,526,000	
Distribution costs	629,000	
Inventory at 31 March 20X3	337,000	
Plant and equipment – cost	2,105,000	
Plant and equipment – accumulated depreciation at 31 March 20X3		
Sales revenue		8,356,000
Vehicles – cost	258,000	
Vehicles – accumulated depreciation at 31 March 20X3		118,000

Additional information:

Non-current assets are depreciated as follows:

- Plant and equipment: 20% per annum straight line
- Vehicles: 25% per annum reducing balance

Depreciation of plant and equipment is charged to cost of sales, and depreciation of vehicles is a distribution cost.

Calculate the amount that would be shown for distribution costs in XCB Co's statement of profit or loss for the year ended 31 March 20X4.

$ 664 000

11 The following information is an extract from the trial balance for XCB Co at 31 March 20X4:

	$	$
Purchases	6,526,000	
Distribution costs	629,000	
Inventory at 31 March 20X3	337,000	
Plant and equipment – cost	2,105,000	
Plant and equipment – accumulated depreciation at 31 March 20X3		
Vehicles - cost	258,000	
Vehicles – accumulated depreciation at 31 March 20X3		118,000

Additional information:

(a)   Non-current assets are depreciated as follows:

- Plant and equipment: 20% per annum straight line
- Vehicles: 25% per annum reducing balance

Depreciation of plant and equipment is charged to cost of sales, and depreciation of vehicles is a distribution cost.

(b)   The closing inventory at 31 March 20X4 was $438,000.

Calculate the amount that would be shown for cost of sales in XCB Co's statement of profit or loss for the year ended 31 March 20X4.

$  6846 000

---

12 The following information is an extract from the trial balance for XCB Co at 31 March 20X4:

	$	$
Warehouse – cost	8,000,000	
Warehouse – accumulated amortisation at 31 March 20X4		1,600,000
Plant and equipment – cost	2,105,000	
Plant and equipment – accumulated depreciation at 31 March 20X3		
Vehicles – cost	258,000	
Vehicles – accumulated depreciation at 31 March 20X3		118,000

Additional information:

Several years ago XCB Co purchased a warehouse which is being depreciated over 20 years on a straight-line basis. In the early part of 20X4, a neighbouring company had performed extensive groundwork on its factory and this destabilised the foundations of XCB Co's building, causing significant cracks to appear in the warehouse. This physical damage prompted XCB Co's directors to carry out an impairment review of the warehouse.

At 31 March 20X4 the warehouse was found to have the following values:

- Value in use: $4,200,000
- Fair value less cost to sell: $3,600,000

Calculate the amount that would be shown as the value of the warehouse in XCB Co's statement of financial position at 31 March 20X4 and the amount of any impairment loss to be recognised in the statement of profit or loss.

Warehouse $ 4 200 000

Impairment loss $ 2 200 000 ✓

---

13 The following information is an extract from the trial balance for XCB Co at 31 March 20X4:

	$	$
Cash and cash equivalents		13,000
Inventory at 31 March 20X3	337,000	
Long-term loan		600,000
Trade payables		470,000
Trade receivables	382,000	

Additional information:

(a) Corporate income tax due for the year ended 31 March 20X4 is estimated at $65,000.

(b) The closing inventory at 31 March 20X4 was $438,000.

Calculate the amounts to be shown as current assets and current liabilities in XCB Co's statement of financial position at 31 March 20X4.

Current assets $ 820 000

Current liabilities $ 548 000 ✓

---

14 An asset is purchased on 1 October 20X0 for $1,400,000. It is to be depreciated using the straight-line basis over 20 years. On 1 October 20X8, the asset is revalued to $1,200,000. The company makes an annual transfer of excess depreciation to the revaluation surplus.

What will be the carrying amount of the asset and the revaluation surplus at the year end 30 September 20X9?

- ○ Non-current asset: $990,910; Revaluation surplus: $400,000
- ○ Non-current asset: $1,100,000; Revaluation surplus: $430,000
- ◉ Non-current asset: $1,100,000; Revaluation surplus: $330,000 ✓
- ○ Non-current asset: $990,910; Revaluation surplus: $430,000

15 FOS Co has built a new factory incurring the following costs:

	$
Land	1,200,000
Materials	2,400,000
Labour	3,000,000
Architect's fees	25,000
Surveyor's fees	15,000
Site preparation costs	300,000
Apportioned administrative overheads	150,000
Testing of fire alarms (legally required)	10,000
Business rates for the first year	12,000
Total	7,112,000

What will be the total amount capitalised in respect of the factory?

○ $6,112,000

◉ $6,950,000   ✓

○ $7,112,000

○ $7,100,000

---

16 WEH Co purchased a machine on 1 July 20X7 for $500,000. It is being depreciated on a straight-line basis over its useful life of ten years. Residual value is estimated at $20,000. On 1 January 20X8, following a change in legislation, WEH Co fitted a safety guard to the machine. The safety guard cost $25,000 and has a useful life of five years with no residual value.

What amount will be charged to profit or loss for the year ended 31 March 20X8 in respect of depreciation on this machine?

$ [   ]

---

17 AUC Co purchased a machine for $60,000 on 1 January 20X7 and assigned it a useful life of 15 years.

On 31 March 20X9 it was revalued to $64,000 with no change in useful life. AUC Co depreciates assets on a monthly basis.

What will be the depreciation charge in relation to this machine in the financial statements of AUC Co for the year ending 31 December 20X9?

$ [   ]

---

18 An asset is hired under a lease with a non-refundable deposit of $20,000 on 1 January 20X1 plus four annual payments in arrears of $40,000 each. The present value of the lease payments (including the $20,000 deposit) is $155,000. The interest rate implicit in the lease is 7%.

What is the finance cost in relation to this lease for the year ending 31 December 20X2? Give your answer to the nearest $.

○ $4,316

⊘ $7,312

○ $8,810

○ $9,450

✓

19 On 1 January 20X1, a lessee leases a non-current asset on a non-cancellable lease contract of five years, the details of which are as follows:

- The asset has a useful life of six years.
- The rental is $21,000 per annum payable at the end of each year.
- The present value of future lease payments is $88,500.
- There is no option to purchase the asset at the end of the lease term.

The interest rate implicit in the lease is 6%.

The current lease liability for the year ended 31 December 20X1 to the nearest $ is:

$ | 16631   ✓

The depreciation charge for the year ended 31 December 20X1 to the nearest $ is:

$ | 14750   ✗

20 CS acquired a machine, using a lease, on 1 January 20X4. The lease was for a five-year term with rentals of $20,000 per year payable in arrears. The present value of future lease payments was $80,000 and the implied interest rate is 8% per year.

What is the non-current lease liability figure required by IFRS 16 *Leases* to be shown in CS's statement of financial position at 31 December 20X5 ? Give your answer to the nearest $.

$ |

21 Palace Co purchased an asset in January 20X1 for $650,000. It was to be depreciated on a straight-line basis over its useful life of ten years. On 1 January 20X5, the company carried out an impairment review as the asset was not performing in line with expectations. It was established that the asset's value in use was $300,000, the cost of a replacement asset would be $360,000, and the fair value less costs of disposal of the asset was $350,000. It was also decided that the total useful life of the asset would be eight years, rather than the original ten.

Calculate the depreciation charge for the asset in the year ended 31 December 20X5.

$ |

22 Teatime Co held a non-current asset at the revalued carrying amount of $260,000 at 30 June 20X6. There was a balance of $60,000 in the revaluation surplus in respect of this asset. An impairment review was carried out at this date under IAS 36 *Impairment of Assets*, and it was found that the value in use of the asset was $190,000, and its fair value less costs of disposal was $180,000.

How much will be debited to the revaluation surplus, and how much to the statement of profit or loss in respect of this impairment?

○ Statement of profit or loss: $20,000; Revaluation surplus: $60,000

○ Statement of profit or loss: $70,000; Revaluation surplus: $0

○ Statement of profit or loss: $0; Revaluation surplus: $70,000

○ Statement of profit or loss: $10,000; Revaluation surplus: $60,000

---

23 IAS 36 *Impairment of Assets* suggests how indications of impairment might be recognised.

Which TWO of the following would be EXTERNAL INDICATORS that one or more of an entity's assets may be impaired?

☐ An unusually significant fall in the market value of one or more assets

☐ Evidence of obsolescence of one or more assets

☐ A decline in the economic performance of one or more assets

☐ An increase in the market interest rates used to calculate value in use of the assets

---

24 On 1 October 20X8, Mash Co decided to sell off part of its business and recognised certain assets as assets held for sale under IFRS 5 *Non-current Assets Held for Sale and Discontinued Operations*.

These assets had been purchased on 1 October 20X4 for $1,400,000. They were to be depreciated on a straight-line basis over 10 years. Their fair value on 1 October 20X8 was $1,000,000, with costs of disposal of $50,000, and their value in use was $1,100,000. Three months later, the assets were sold for $1,250,000.

What is the gain or loss on disposal?

◉ $410,000 gain ✓

○ $300,000 gain

○ $150,000 loss

○ $150,000 gain

---

25 On 1 June 20X6 the directors of DP commissioned a report to determine possible actions they could take to reduce DP's losses.

The report was presented to the directors on 1 December 20X6 and proposed that DP cease all of its manufacturing activities and concentrate on its retail activities. The directors formally approved the plan to close DP's factory. The factory was gradually shut down, commencing on 5 December 20X6, with production finally ceasing on 15 March 20X7.

All employees had ceased working or had been transferred to other facilities in the company by 29 March 20X7. Plant and equipment which had a carrying amount of $95,000 was removed and sold for $25,000 on 30 March 20X7.

The factory and building are being advertised for sale but had not been sold by 31 March 20X7. The carrying amount of the land and building at 31 March 20X7, based on original cost, was $750,000. The estimated net realisable value of the land and building at 31 March 20X7 was $1,125,000.

The manufacturing activities reported a loss for the year ended 31 March 20X7 of $700,000 and closure costs incurred (and paid) up to 31 March 20X7 were $620,000.

The cash flows, revenues and expenses relating to the factory were clearly distinguishable from DP's other operations. The output of the factory was sold directly to third parties and to DP's retail outlets. The manufacturing facility was shown as a separate segment in DP's segmental information.

Calculate the loss that should be disclosed on the statement of profit or loss and other comprehensive income for the year ended 31 March 20X7, assuming that DP makes the minimum disclosure required in relation to IFRS 5 *Non-current Assets Held for Sale and Discontinued Operations.*

$ [   ]

---

26 Company Y closed one of its divisions nine months ago. It has yet to dispose of one remaining machine. The carrying amount of the machine at the date when business ceased was $600,000 and it was being depreciated at 20% on a reducing balance basis. Company Y has been advised that the fair value of the machine is $610,000 and expects to incur costs of $20,000 in making the sale. It has located a probable buyer but the sale will not be completed before the year end.

Where should the carrying amount of the machine be shown in Company Y's statement of financial position?

○ Under non-current assets

○ Under current assets

○ Included within inventory

○ Included within receivables

---

27 Closing inventories are shown at a cost of $485,000. Of these, inventories costing $48,000 are found to have been damaged. They can only be sold for 75% of the usual $60,000 selling price, and the company would incur further costs of $4,000 in remedial work.

What value should be shown for inventories at the year end in the company's statement of financial position?

○ $41,000

○ $485,000

◉ $478,000

○ $482,000

---

28   Place a tick in the relevant box to show whether the following statements about IAS 2 *Inventories* are correct or incorrect.

	Correct	Incorrect
Production overheads should be included in cost on the basis of a company's actual level of activity in the period.		
In arriving at the net realisable value of inventories, settlement discounts must be deducted from the expected selling price.		
In arriving at the cost of inventories, FIFO, LIFO and weighted average cost formulas are acceptable.		
It is permitted to value finished goods inventories at materials plus labour cost only, without adding production overheads.		

29   Which ONE of the following events taking place after the year end but before the financial statements were authorised for issue would require adjustment in accordance with IAS 10 *Events after the Reporting Period*?

- O Three lines of inventory held at the year end were destroyed by flooding in the warehouse.

- O The directors announced a major restructuring.

- O Two lines of inventory held at the year end were discovered to have faults rendering them unsaleable.

- O The value of the company's investments fell sharply.

30   Which TWO of the following events occurring after the reporting date of a company but before the financial statements are authorised for issue are classified as adjusting events in accordance with IAS 10 *Events after the Reporting Period*?

- ☐ A change in tax rate announced after the reporting date, but affecting the current tax liability

- ☑ The discovery of a fraud which had occurred during the year

- ☐ The determination of the sale proceeds of an Item of plant sold before the year end

- ☐ The damage of one section of a factory by fire

31   The following is an extract from the statement of financial position of Falcon at 31 December 20X8:

	20X8 $	20X7 $
Property, plant and equipment	774,000	847,000
Revaluation surplus	580,000	500,000

During the year ended 31 December 20X8, the company purchased new plant costing $121,000 and revalued land from $25,000 to $105,000. The company also sold some assets for $68,000, making a gain on disposal of $14,000.

According to the requirements of IAS 7 Statements of Cash Flows, what is the figure for depreciation to be adjusted in the operating activities section of the statement of cash flows for the year ended 31 December 20X8?

○ $140,000

○ $220,000

○ $206,000

○ $260,000

---

32 **Which of the following items are included in the statement of cash flows under the heading 'cash flows from investing activities'?**

☑ Interest received

☐ Non-equity dividends paid

☐ Equity dividends paid

☐ Repayment of borrowings

☑ Dividends received

---

33 The statement of financial position of PNT Co at 31 January 20X7 showed property, plant and equipment with a carrying amount of $1,860,000. At 31 January 20X8 it had increased to $2,880,000.

During the year to 31 March 20X8 plant with a carrying amount of $240,000 was sold at a loss of $90,000, depreciation of $280,000 was charged and $100,000 was added to the revaluation surplus in respect of property, plant and equipment.

What amount should appear under 'investing activities' in the statement of cash flows of PNT Co for the year ended 31 January 20X8 as cash paid to acquire property, plant and equipment?

○ $1,640,000

⊘ $1,440,000

○ $1,260,000

○ $1,350,000

---

34 A company's sales revenue for the year just ended was $28 million. The company earned a gross margin of 40% on sales. All sales and purchases were on credit. The following balances have been extracted from the year-end accounts:

	$m
Inventory	4
Trade receivables	6
Trade payables	3

Calculate, to the nearest day, the company's cash operating cycle based on the year-end figures.

| 100 | days ✓

---

35 **The effective incidence of a tax is:**

○ The date the tax is actually paid

◉ The person or entity that finally bears the cost of the tax

○ The date the tax assessment is issued ✓

○ The person or entity paying the tax authority

---

36 **Which TWO of the following are likely to be a source of tax rules in a country?**

☐ International Financial Reporting Standards

☐ Corporate governance

☐ International organisations such as the European Union

☐ Interpretations issued by the IFRS Interpretations Committee

☐ Domestic legislation and court rulings

---

37 RWS sells goods to customers on credit. It is forecast that credit sales for January will be $52,000 and that sales will increase by $4,000 per month for the next four months. Based on past experience RWS expects 60% of customers to pay in the month after sale, 20% of customers to pay two months after sale and 15% to pay three months after sale with 5% of sales not being collected.

RWS has a trade receivables balance outstanding at the beginning of January of $42,000.

Calculate the cash that RWS will receive from credit customers during the four-month period to the end of April.

| $ | |

---

38 The following budgeted information has been prepared by YHN for the last quarter of the year:

	October	November	December
Opening inventory (units)	100	140	120
Closing inventory (units)	140	120	150
Sales (units)	420	460	450

Materials cost $3 per unit.

40% of purchases are paid for immediately in cash while the other 60% are purchased on credit and are paid two months after purchase.

Calculate budgeted payments in December for the purchase of materials.

| $ | 1404 | ✓

39 **Which one of the following would NOT be a viable solution to overcome a forecast short-term cash deficit?**

- ○ Reducing inventory levels as far as possible
- ○ Bringing forward supplier payments to obtain settlement discounts
- ○ Negotiating a higher overdraft limit with the bank
- ○ Delaying non-essential capital expenditure

40 **Which TWO of the following are statutory powers that a tax authority may be granted to ensure compliance with tax regulations?**

- ☐ Power to arrest individuals
- ☐ Power of entry and search of premises
- ☐ Power to exchange information with other tax authorities
- ☐ Power to confiscate assets of the entity

41 The government of Country X has estimated the following for the year ended 31 December 20X4:

- Total income tax due: $166 billion
- Total income tax expected to be collected: $135 billion
- Income tax that will not be collected due to tax evasion: $10 billion
- Income tax that will not be collected due to tax avoidance: $15 billion

The 'tax gap' for the year to 31 December 20X4 is expected to be:

- ○ $6 billion
- ○ $16 billion
- ○ $21 billion
- ○ $31 billion

42 **Which one of the following correctly describes the meaning of 'rollover relief'?**

- ○ A trading loss that can be carried forward and used to reduce tax in a future profitable year
- ○ A capital loss incurred on the disposal of an asset that can be carried forward to a future tax year
- ○ An entity ceasing to trade, carrying back a trading loss to set off against previous years' profits
- ○ A gain arising from the sale of an asset that is deferred provided the entity reinvests the proceeds of the sale in a replacement asset

43 YZ is incorporated in Country X where the rate of corporate income tax on profits and capital gains is 25%.

YZ purchased a non-depreciable asset for $45,000 on 1 January 20X5 and incurred additional purchase costs of $5,000.

The asset was eventually sold for $110,000 on 31 December 20X9.

The indexation factor from 1 January 20X5 to 31 December 20X9 was 35%.

BPP
LEARNING
MEDIA

What is the capital gains tax that YZ is due to pay on the disposal of the asset?

- ○ $10,625
- ○ $16,250
- ○ $42,500
- ○ $60,000

---

44 YJ uses factoring to manage its trade receivables. The factor advances 75% of invoiced sales and charges interest at a rate of 13% per annum. YJ has estimated sales revenue for next year of $2,500,000. The average time for the factor to receive payment from customers is 45 days.

Calculate the estimated interest charge payable to the factor for next year. Give your answer to the nearest $.

$ [   ]

---

45 YRS, an entity resident in Country X, had an accounting profit for the year ended 30 June 20X7 of $2,580,000. The accounting profit was after charging depreciation of $126,000 and a political donation of $45,000.

YRS was entitled to a tax depreciation allowance of $153,000 for the year to 30 June 20X7.

Relevant tax rules

Corporate profits

The rules for taxation of corporate profits are as follows:

- Accounting rules of recognition and measurement are followed for tax purposes.
- All expenses other than depreciation, amortisation, entertaining, taxes paid to other public bodies and donations to political parties are tax deductible.
- The corporate tax on profits is at a rate of 25%.

What is YRS's tax payable for the year ended 30 June 20X7?

- ○ $606,750
- ○ $619,500
- ○ $638,250
- ✓ $649,500   ✓

---

46 YKI is a retailer of decorative birdcages. One particular birdcage design has an annual demand of 12,000 units and demand is spread evenly throughout the year.

The cost of each birdcage to YKI is $24. Ordering costs are $100 and the annual cost of holding one birdcage in inventory is estimated to be $2.

Calculate the economic order quantity (EOQ) for the birdcage to the nearest unit.

[346.] units   ✗ calc error

116

47   SB is resident in Country X and is considering starting business activities in a foreign country. An entity may conduct a foreign operation through a branch or a subsidiary.

Which ONE of the following is an advantage of SB operating its foreign operation as a subsidiary?

    ○   A loss made by the foreign operation will be available to the SB group.

    ⊘   SB will only pay tax on dividends received from its foreign operation.

    ○   All profits/losses overseas will be subject to tax in Country X.

    ○   SB can claim tax depreciation on its foreign operation's assets.   ✓

---

48   BH purchased 250 items of a product from a foreign entity and imported them into Country X. On import, the products were subject to an excise duty of $8 per item and sales tax (VAT) at the standard rate of 15% on the cost including the excise duty.

BH purchased the items for $45 each and after importing them sold all of the items for $65 each plus sales tax (VAT) at the standard rate of 15%.

How much is due to be paid by BH to the tax authorities in total for these transactions? Give your answer to the nearest $.

    ○ $450

    ⊘ $2,450   ✓

    ○ $2,750

    ○ $3,988

---

49   Country X is considering levying an excise duty of $1,000 per vehicle on all new motor vehicles sold.

Which TWO of the following taxes would be regarded as a correct description of the $1,000 excise duty?

    ☐   A progressive tax

    ☐   An indirect tax

    ☐   An ad valorum tax

    ☐   A regressive tax

    ☐   A unit tax

---

50   An entity has an aggressive policy for financing working capital.

This means that short-term funding is used to fund:

    ○   Part of the fluctuating net current assets and none of the permanent part of net current assets

    ○   Part of the fluctuating net current assets and part of the permanent part of net current assets

    ⊘   All of the fluctuating net current assets and part of the permanent part of net current assets   ✓

    ○   All of the fluctuating net current assets and all of the permanent part of net current assets

---

51 QR is resident in a country that uses the classical system for the taxation of entity profits paid to shareholders as dividends. Corporate income tax on profits is charged at 25%.

QR made a taxable profit for the year to 31 December 20X3 of $200,000 and paid a dividend of $75,000. The shareholders pay income tax of 20% on dividends received.

Calculate the corporate income tax paid by QR on its profits and the tax paid by the shareholders in respect of the dividend of $75,000.

Tax paid by QR	$	

Tax paid by shareholders	$	

52 AB is preparing its cash budget for the next quarter.

Which of the following items should NOT be included in the cash budget?

○ Payment of tax due on last year's profits

○ Gain on the disposal of a piece of machinery

○ Repayment of the capital amount of a loan

○ Receipt of interest from short-term investments

53 The tax rules of Country X allow an entity ceasing to trade to carry back terminal losses against the previous two years' profits. Corporate income tax on profits is at a rate of 25%.

CT ceased trading on 31 March 20X4, having incurred a trading loss of $75,000 for the year ended 31 March 20X4.

CT's profits for the previous three years were as follows:

Year to 31 March	Taxable trading profit
20X1	$95,000
20X2	$40,000
20X3	$25,000

Assuming that CT had paid all tax due up to 31 March 20X3, calculate the tax refund that CT can claim for its terminal loss.

$ 16,250 ✓

54 **Which ONE of the following best describes a bond?**

Ⓧ A negotiable instrument offering a fixed rate of interest over a fixed period of time and with a fixed redemption value ✓

○ A negotiable instrument which provides evidence of a fixed term deposit with a bank; maturity is normally within 90 days but can be longer

○ A document which sets out a commitment to pay a sum of money at a specified point in time

○ An unsecured short-term loan note issued by companies and generally maturing within a period of up to one year

55 Which ONE of the following correctly describes a certificate of deposit?

- ○ A debt instrument which offers a fixed rate of interest over a fixed period of time and with a fixed redemption value
- ◉ A negotiable instrument which provides evidence of a fixed term deposit with a bank
- ○ A document which sets out a commitment to deposit a sum of money at a specified point in time
- ○ A certificate which shows ownership of part of the share capital of a company ✓

56 Which THREE of the following are features of a Treasury bill?

- ☑ Treasury bills are issued at a discount to their face value.
- ☐ Treasury bills are issued by banks.
- ☐ Treasury bills are low risk and low return investments. —
- ☑ Treasury bills have a maturity of less than one year. ✓
- ☑ Treasury bills are not negotiable instruments. ✗

57 A company is considering offering its customers an early settlement discount. The company currently receives payments from customers on average 65 days after the invoice date. The company is considering offering a 2% early settlement discount for payment within 30 days of the invoice date.

What is the effective annual interest rate of the early settlement discount using compound interest methodology and assuming a 365-day year?

- ○ 22.94%
- ○ 20.86%
- ◉ 23.45%
- ○ 27.85% ✓

58 The economic order quantity (EOQ) is the order quantity which results in:

- ○ The lowest cost of ordering inventory
- ○ The highest discount from suppliers
- ○ The lowest combined total costs of ordering and holding inventory
- ○ The lowest cost of holding inventory

59 CTA Co is reviewing its working capital management.

Which TWO of the following statements concerning working capital management are correct?

- ☑ The twin objectives of working capital management are profitability and liquidity.
- ☐ A conservative approach to working capital investment will increase profitability.
- ☑ Working capital management is a key factor in a company's long-term success.
- ☐ Liquid assets give the highest returns leading to conflicts of objectives. ✓

60   The management of RKU Co is considering an aggressive approach to financing working capital.

Which of the following statements relate to an aggressive approach to financing working capital management?

(1)   All non-current assets, permanent current assets and part of fluctuating current assets are financed by long-term funding.

(2)   There is an increased risk of liquidity and cash flow problems.

○   Statement 1 only

◉   Statement 2 only

○   Both statements 1 and 2

○   Neither statement

Practice mock answers

Answers

1   The correct answers are:

- Annual reports should state whether a company has complied with the provisions of the Act and, if they haven't, provide an explanation.

- All members of audit committees should be independent and at least two members should be financial experts.

The Sarbanes–Oxley Act 2002 requires that companies covered by the Act must comply with its provisions. Failure to do so is a criminal offence.

As in the UK, only one member of the audit committee is required to have previous financial experience and expertise.

2   The correct answer is: IFRS Advisory Council.

The IFRS Advisory Council provides advice to the International Accounting Standards Board (IASB) as to the priority areas it should focus on and also advises on major standard setting projects.

It also consults with national standard setters, academics, user groups and other interested parties and informs the IASB of its views on a range of issues.

The IFRS Interpretations Committee prepares interpretations of IFRSs to help businesses apply IFRSs to their financial statements. These are then approved by the IASB. The committee also provides guidance on accounting issues which are not specifically covered by accounting standards.

The International Organization of Securities Commissions (IOSCO) represents the world's securities markets regulators and seeks to encourage and promote the improvement and quality of IFRSs so that multinational companies can use international accounting standards when they list their securities overseas.

The IFRS Foundation oversees the regulation of the accounting profession. It appoints the members of the IASB, IFRS Advisory Council and the IFRS Interpretations Committee and reviews the budgets and strategies of the other organisations.

3   The correct answer is:

- The board should undertake a formal and rigorous evaluation of its own performance and that of its committees and individual directors at least every five years

The UK Corporate Governance Code states that the evaluation should be undertaken annually.

4   The correct answer is: Work with the IASB to develop a common conceptual framework in the long term to ensure future convergence of international standards.

This is the approach taken by the US Financial Accounting Standards Board. Although this process means that in the future international standards should converge, based on the same or similar principles, the US has not 'adopted' international accounting standards.

5   The correct answer is: It promotes the International Accounting Standards Board, its work and the use of IFRS.

6   The correct answers are:

- Self-interest
- Integrity

Priti will personally benefit from the manipulation, which is therefore in her interest, and preparing fair and accurate accounts is an example of the integrity expected of CIMA members and students.

7   The correct answers are:

Fundamental qualitative characteristics	Enhancing qualitative characteristics
Relevance	Comparability
Faithful representation	Verifiability
	Timeliness
	Understandability

8   The correct answer is: The amount of cash that would need to be paid in order to acquire an equivalent asset today.

This measurement base is commonly used where a country has a very high rate of inflation, such that the historic cost basis would give an unrealistic representation of the value of the company's assets.

The net amount of cash expected to be received from selling an asset would be the realisable value of the asset, and is commonly used where the company is intending to get the benefit from its assets by selling them rather than from continuing use; for example, where a company is going into liquidation.

The amount of cash needed to acquire a new asset today would not give a realistic value for the asset held, as it would not reflect the use of the asset by the company to date.

The amount of cash needed in today's money that would need to be paid to acquire an asset in 20 years' time would represent the discounted cost of the asset.

9   The correct answer is: Current cost.

According to the *Conceptual Framework*, the historical cost of an asset is the costs incurred in acquiring/creating the asset plus transactions costs.

The fair value is the price that would be received to sell an asset or paid to transfer a liability in an orderly transaction between market participants at the measurement date.

Value in use is the present value of the cash flows, or other economic benefits, that an entity expects to derive from the use of an asset and from its ultimate disposal.

10 The correct answer is: $664,000.

	$
Distribution costs (per trial balance extract)	629,000
Vehicle depreciation ([258,000 – 118,000] × 25%)	35,000
Total	664,000

11 The correct answer is: $6,846,000.

	$
Opening inventory at 31 March 20X3	337,000
Purchases	6,526,000
Closing inventory at 31 March 20X4	(438,000)
Plant and equipment depreciation (2,105,000 × 25%)	421,000
Total	6,846,000

12   The correct answers are:

Warehouse $4,200,000
Impairment loss $2,200,000

At 31 March 20X4, the carrying amount of the warehouse was $6,400,000 ($8,000,000 – $1,600,000).

It would appear that the warehouse suffered an impairment loss during the early part of 20X4.

The warehouse should be valued at the lower of its current carrying amount ($6,400,000) and its recoverable amount.

The recoverable amount is the higher of the warehouse's fair value less costs of disposal ($3,600,000) and its value in use ($4,200,000).

Therefore the warehouse should be valued at $4,200,000 in the statement of financial position and an impairment loss of $2,200,000 should be recognised in the statement of profit or loss ($6,400,000 – $4,200,000).

13   The correct answer is:

Current assets $820,000
Current liabilities $548,000

	$
Current assets	
Inventory (note (b))	438,000
Trade receivables	382,000
	820,000
Current liabilities	
Bank overdraft (cash and cash equivalents)	13,000
Trade payables	470,000
Current tax payable (note (a))	65,000
	548,000

14   The correct answer is: Non-current asset: $1,100,000; Revaluation surplus: $330,000.

	Non-current asset $	Revaluation surplus $
1 October 20X0 – cost	1,400,000	
Depreciation ($1,400,000/20 years) = $70,000 × 8 years	(560,000)	
Carrying amount – 30 September 20X8	840,000	
Revaluation	360,000	360,000
Carrying amount – 1 October 20X8	1,200,000	
Depreciation ($1,200,000/12 years left)	(100,000)	
Excess depreciation ($100,000 – $70,000)		(30,000)
Carrying amount at 30 September 20X9	1,100,000	330,000

15 The correct answer is: $6,950,000.

	$
Land	1,200,000
Materials	2,400,000
Labour	3,000,000
Architect's fees	25,000
Surveyor's fees	15,000
Site preparation costs	300,000
Testing of fire alarms (legally required)	10,000
Total	6,950,000

16 The correct answer is: $37,250.

	$
Machine ($500,000 – $20,000) × 10 × 9/12)	36,000
Safety guard ($25,000/5 years × 3/12)	1,250
	37,250

17 The correct answer is: $4,765.

The machine has been owned for 2 years 3 months, so the remaining useful life at 31 March 20X9 was 12 years 9 months.

Prior to revaluation it was being depreciated at $4,000 pa ($60,000/15 years), so the charge for the first three months of 20X9 was $1,000.

The machine will now be depreciated over the remaining 12 years 9 months = 153 months. So the charge for the remaining 9 months of 20X9 is $3,765 (($64,000/153 months) × 9 months).

So total depreciation for the year ended 31.12.X9 is (1,000 + 3,765) = $4,765.

18 The correct answer is: $7,312.

Lease liability

		$
1.1.X1	PV of future lease payments	135,000
1.1.X1–31.12.X1	Finance cost (Interest: 7% × 135,000)	9,450
31.12.X1	Instalment	(40,000)
31.12.X1	Liability c/d	104,450
1.1.X2–31.12.X2	Finance cost (Interest: 7% × 104,450)	7,312

Note. The initial measurement of the lease liability is at the present value of future lease payments (lease payments not paid at the commencement date). The $20,000 deposit is a payment made at the commencement date and should therefore be excluded from the initial lease liability. The present value of the lease payments of $155,000 given in the question includes the $20,000 deposit so this must be deducted to arrive at the present value of future lease payments.

The other answers are incorrect for the following reasons:

$4,316 is the answer you would have arrived at if you had incorrectly deducted an instalment each year before calculating the interest. As the payments are in arrears, interest should be calculated before deducting the instalment each year.

$8,810 is the answer you would have arrived at if you forgot to deduct the deposit of $20,000 to arrive at the present value of future lease payments for the opening lease liability on 1 January 20X1.

$9,450 is the finance cost (interest) for 20X1 but the question asked you for the finance cost (interest) for 20X2.

19   The correct answers are:

Current lease liability $16,631
Depreciation charge $17,700

Workings

1   *Lease liability*

	$
1.1.X1	88,500
Finance cost (Interest: 6% × 88,500)	5,310
Instalment in arrears	(21,000)
31.12.X1	72,810
Finance cost (Interest: 6% × 72,810)	4,369
Instalment in arrears	(21,000)
Non-current liability	56,179
Current liability $72,810 – $56,179 =	$16,631

2   *Depreciation*

Depreciate from the commencement date (1.1.X1) to the earlier of the end of the asset's useful life (six years) and the end of the lease term (five years). So here, depreciate over five years.

Depreciation = $88,500/5 years

= $17,700

20   The correct answer is: $35,849.

		$
1.1.X4	PV of future lease payments	80,000
1.1.X4–31.12.X4	Finance cost (Interest: 8% × 80,000)	6,400
31.12.X4	Instalment (in arrears)	(20,000)
31.12.X4	Liability c/d	66,400
1.1.X5–31.12.X5	Finance cost (Interest: 8% × 66,400)	5,312
31.12.X5	Instalment in arrears	(20,000)
31.12.X5	**Liability c/d**	**51,712**
1.1.X6–31.12.X6	Finance cost (Interest: 8% × 51,712)	4,137
31.12.X6	Instalment in arrears	(20,000)
	Non-current liability	**35,849**
Current liability	(51,712 – 35,849)	15,863
Non-current liability		35,849
Total balance at 31.12.X5		51,712

21 The correct answer is: $87,500.

	$
Purchase cost – 1 January 20X1	650,000
Depreciation for X1, X2, X3 and X4 ($650,000/10 years × 4 years)	(260,000)
Carrying amount – 31 December 20X4	390,000

1 January 20X5 the recoverable amount is the higher of:

Value in use – $300,000

Fair value less costs of disposal – $350,000

New carrying amount at 1 January 20X5	350,000
Depreciation ($350,000/(8 years – 4 years))	87,500

22 The correct answer is: Statement of profit or loss: $10,000; Revaluation surplus: $60,000.

The recoverable amount is the higher of the value in use and the fair value less costs of disposal of the asset – therefore $190,000.

This is $70,000 less than the carrying amount, and therefore the impairment loss is $70,000.

The $60,000 in the revaluation surplus should be reduced to nil, and the remaining $10,000 of loss should be recognised as an expense in the statement of profit or loss.

23 The correct answes are:

- An unusually significant fall in the market value of one or more assets
- An increase in the market interest rates used to calculate value in use of the assets

The other two options are internal indicators of impairment rather than external indicators.

24 The correct answer is: $410,000 gain.

	$'000
Cost of assets – 1 October 20X4	1,400
Depreciation ($1,400,000/10 years × 4 years)	(560)
Carrying amount – 30 September 20X8	840

The fair value less costs of disposal of $950,000 is higher than the carrying amount; therefore the asset will be transferred at $840,000.

	$'000
Sale proceeds	1,250
Carrying amount	(840)
Gain on disposal	410

When an asset is classified as 'held for sale' it should be remeasured to the lower of its current carrying amount ($840,000) and its fair value less costs of disposal ($950,000 [$1,000,000 – $50,000]).

At this point no further depreciation is charged on the asset – it is simply held at its carrying amount of $840,000 until it is disposed of, at which point a gain or loss on disposal is calculated.

25 The correct answer is: $1,390,000.

In the statement of profit or loss and other comprehensive income one figure will be shown under discontinued operations, being the trading loss for the period from the discontinued operation ($700,000), plus the loss on disposal of the plant and equipment ($70,000), plus the closure costs ($620,000). This single figure should then be analysed in the notes.

26 The correct answer is: Under current assets.

Non-current assets held for sale are shown separately under the 'current assets' heading.

27 The correct answer is: $478,000.

	$
Expected selling price ($60,000 × 75%)	45,000
Cost of extra remedial work	(4,000)
Net realisable value	41,000

This is $7,000 lower than the cost price of $48,000.

Therefore the difference of $7,000 must be deducted from the inventories amount of $485,000 in order to show inventories at a value of $478,000.

28 The correct answer is:

	Correct	Incorrect
Production overheads should be included in cost on the basis of a company's actual level of activity in the period.		☑
In arriving at the net realisable value of inventories, settlement discounts must be deducted from the expected selling price.		☑
In arriving at the cost of inventories, FIFO, LIFO and weighted average cost formulas are acceptable.		☑
It is permitted to value finished goods inventories at materials plus labour cost only, without adding production overheads.		☑

Production overheads are allocated on the basis of a company's **normal** level of activity.

Settlement discounts are not deducted to arrive at NRV.

The LIFO formula is not allowed under IAS 2 *Inventories*.

Valuation of finished goods should include production overheads.

29 The correct answer is: Two lines of inventory held at the year end were discovered to have faults rendering them unsaleable.

We can assume that these faults also existed at the year end, so this is the only option which would require adjustment. The others have all taken place after the year end and so would be disclosed as a non-adjusting event if deemed material.

30 The correct answers are:

- The discovery of a fraud which occurred during the year
- The determination of the sale proceeds of an item of plant sold before the year end

These both provide evidence of conditions that existed at the end of the reporting period. The other options refer to conditions which arose after the reporting period and are therefore non-adjusting events according to IAS 10 *Events after the Reporting Period*.

31 The correct answer is: $220,000.

	$
PPE brought forward	847,000
Additions	121,000
Revaluation surplus (105 − 25)	80,000
Disposal (68 − 14 = carrying amount 54)	(54,000)
Balancing figure = depreciation	(220,000)
PPE carried forward	774,000

32 The correct answers are:

- Interest received
- Dividends received

Dividends paid are included either as operating activities or cash flows from financing activities.

The repayment of borrowings would be disclosed within financing activities.

33 The correct answer is: $1,440,000.

	$
Balance b/f − 1 February 20X7	1,860,000
Revaluation during the year	100,00
Disposal during the year	(240,000)
Depreciation charge for the year	(280,000)
Subtotal	1,440,000
Therefore, additions during the year (bal. figure)	1,440,000
Balance c/f − 31 January 20X8	2,880,000

34 The correct answer is: 100 days.

	Days
Inventory days ((4/[28 × 60%]) × 365 days)	87
Trade receivable days (6/28 × 365 days)	78
Trade payable days ((3/[28 × 60%]) × 365 days)	(65)
Cash operating cycle	100

35 The correct answer is: The person or entity that finally bears the cost of the tax.

The effective incidence falls on the individual or entity that bears the end cost of a tax. In the case of sales tax this would be the end consumer.

The formal incidence falls on the individual or entity that has direct contact with the tax authorities. This is usually the company as it must account for the sales tax and pay it over to the tax authorities.

36   The correct answers are:

- International organisations such as the European Union
- Domestic legislation and court rulings

The main sources of tax rules tend to come from:

- Domestic legislation and court rulings (case law)

- International organisations, such as the European Union (also known as 'supranational bodies')

- Past practice of local tax authorities

- Agreements between different countries, such as double taxation treaties

37   The correct answer is: $170,100.

This is calculated as:

	Jan $	Feb $	Mar $	April $
Sales	52,000	56,000	60,000	64,000
60% received after 1 month		31,200	33,600	36,000
20% received after 2 months			10,400	11,200
15% received after 3 months				7,800
5% not collected				

Opening bal paid Jan, Feb, March (less 5% not collected)	42,000			
	39,900	31,200	44,000	55,000

Total cash received	=	$39,000 + $31,200 + $44,000 + $55,000
	=	$170,100

38   The correct answer is: $1,404.

	October	November	December
Sales (units)	420	460	450
Less opening inventory	(100)	(140)	(120)
Plus closing inventory	140	120	150
Units purchased	460	440	480
Cost @ $3	$1,380	$1,320	$1,440

	$
Re October: 60% × $1,380	828
Re December: 40% × $1,440	576
	1,404

39 The correct answer is: Bringing forward supplier payments to obtain settlement discounts.

This would require suppliers to be paid earlier than scheduled which would immediately worsen the cash deficit.

40 The correct answers are:

- Power of entry and search of premises
- Power to exchange information with other tax authorities

Other powers that a tax authority may be granted include:

- Power to review and query returns submitted to them
- Power to request special reports or returns
- Power to examine records which support returns made

41 The 'tax gap' describes the difference between the tax a tax authority should collect and what it actually collects.

	$bn
Total income tax due	166
Less tax expected to be collected	(135)
Tax gap	31

42 The correct answer is: A gain arising from the sale of an asset that is deferred provided the entity reinvests the proceeds of the sale in a replacement asset.

Rollover relief effectively defers the capital gains tax payable by an entity on the disposal of a non-current asset to a future period provided that the sales proceeds received are used to buy a replacement asset no tax will be due on the capital gain.

43 The correct answer is: $10,625.

	$
Purchase price	45,000
Additional purchase costs	5,000
Original cost	50,000
Sales proceeds	110,000
Less: original cost	50,000
indexation allowance on original cost ($50,000 × 35%)	17,500
Capital gain	42,500
Tax at 25% on capital gain	10,625

44 The correct answer is: $30,051.

The factor will advance 75% of annual sales: 75% × $2,500,000 = $1,875,000.

The funds advanced will incur interest until the factor collects the money from the customers.

Trade receivables = 45/365 × $1,875,000 = $231,164

Interest at 13% = $231,164 × 13% = $30,051

45   The correct answer is: $649,500.

This is calculated as follows:

	$
Accounting profit	2,580,000
Add: depreciation	126,000
political donation	45,000
	2,751,000
Less tax depreciation	(153,000)
Taxable profit	2,598,000
Tax payable ($2,598,000 × 25%)	649,500

46   The correct answer is: 1,095 units.

$$EOQ = \sqrt{\frac{2CoD}{Ch}}$$

$$EOQ = \sqrt{\frac{2 \times \$100 \times 12,000}{\$2}}$$

EOQ = 1,095 units

47   The correct answer is: SB will only pay tax on dividends received from its foreign operation.

SB will pay tax on its worldwide income in Country X (where it is resident). If SB operates its foreign operation as a subsidiary the subsidiary will pay tax in the country where it is resident. Therefore SB will only pay tax on the funds remitted to it in the form of a dividend from its subsidiary.

48   The correct answer is: $2,450.

	$
Sales tax (VAT) due on sales ($65 × 15% × 250 items)	2,438
Sales tax (VAT) suffered on purchases ([$45 + $8] × 15% × 250 items)	1,988
Sales tax (VAT) payable	450
Excise duty (250 items × $8)	2,000
Total tax due	2,450

49   The correct answers are:

- An indirect tax
- A unit tax

An indirect tax is a tax on expenditure and one that is levied on one person or entity with the intention that the tax burden is passed on to another person/entity.

A unit tax is an example of an indirect tax and is based on the number or weight of items (here $1,000 per motor vehicle).

A progressive tax is a direct tax where an increasing proportion of income is taken in tax as income rises.

An ad valorem tax is an example of an indirect tax and is based on the value of the item (for example, sales tax (VAT)). Here the excise duty is $1,000 regardless of the value of the motor vehicle and so it is not an ad valorem tax.

A regressive tax is a direct tax where a decreasing proportion of income is taken in tax as income rises.

50   The correct answer is: All of the fluctuating net current assets and part of the permanent part of net current assets.

Three possible policies exist to finance working capital:

Conservative policy – all of the permanent assets (current and non-current) and some of the fluctuating current assets are financed by long-term funding.

Aggressive policy – all of the fluctuating and part of the permanent current assets are financed by short-term funding.

Moderate policy – short-term funding is used to finance the fluctuating current assets and the permanent assets (current and non-current) are financed by long-term funding.

51   The correct answers are:

- Tax paid by QR: $50,000
- Tax paid by shareholders: $15,000

Under the classical system, companies and individuals are treated separately for taxation purposes. This means that the profits are effectively taxed twice.

	$
Tax on QR's profits ($200,000 × 25%)	50,000
Tax on dividends ($75,000 × 20%)	15,000

52   The correct answer is: Gain on the disposal of a piece of machinery.

A cash budget forecasts the cash inflows and cash outflows of an organisation for a period of time and must therefore only include cash flows.

The gain on disposal of a piece of machinery is the difference between the sales proceeds and the carrying amount of the asset in the statement of financial position and is not a cash flow. The sales proceeds are, however, a cash flow and should be included in the cash budget.

53   The correct answer is: $16,250.

	$
Terminal loss offset against taxable profits in 20X3	25,000
Terminal loss offset against taxable profits in 20X2	40,000
No terminal loss offset against taxable profits in 20X1 as carry back only available for 2 years	0
	65,000
Tax refund ($65,000 × 25%)	16,250

54   The correct answer is: A negotiable instrument offering a fixed rate of interest over a fixed period of time and with a fixed redemption value.

Bonds tend to carry a fixed rate of interest and have a specific term. They are negotiable as they can be traded and sold by one party to another.

55 The correct answer is: A negotiable instrument which provides evidence of a fixed term deposit with a bank.

Certificates of deposit are used where an entity has a significant amount of funds to invest for a fixed term. The investing entity can hold on to the debt instrument until maturity or it can sell it on at a discount if it needs the funds before the maturity date as the instrument is negotiable.

Certificates of deposit usually pay a fixed rate of interest.

56 The correct answers are:

- Treasury bills are issued at a discount to their face value.
- Treasury bills are low risk and low return investments.
- Treasury bills have a maturity of less than one year.

Treasury bills are negotiable instruments issued by the government. They have a maturity of less than one year (typically 91 days).

There are redeemable at face value and there is a large and active secondary market in treasury bills meaning that they are easily traded (negotiable) if funds are required before the maturity date.

57 The correct answer is: 23.45%.

$$\text{Effective 'early settlement' interest rate} = \left(\frac{100}{100 - \text{discount}}\right)^{\frac{365}{\text{days early}}} - 1$$

$$= \left(\frac{100}{100 - 2}\right)^{\frac{365}{(65 - 30)}} - 1$$

$$= \left(\frac{100}{98}\right)^{\frac{365}{35}} - 1$$

$$= 23.45\%$$

58 The correct answer is: The lowest combined total costs of ordering and holding inventory.

The economic order quantity model tells a business how many units of inventory it should order each time it places an order so that the business can minimise annual inventory costs (cost of ordering and holding inventory).

59 The correct answers are:

- The twin objectives of working capital management are profitability and liquidity.
- Working capital management is a key factor in a company's long-term success.

Statement 1 is correct because sufficient working capital should be maintained to ensure bills can be paid on time. However, working capital (receivables, inventory, payables) do not earn a return as such, so excessive working capital is undesirable – spare cash, for example, should be temporarily placed to earn a return (provided risk is low).

Statement 2 is incorrect. A conservative approach to working capital investment implies aiming to keep relatively high levels of working capital. The reason for this is generally to reduce risk (less risk of inventory shortages, give customers plenty of time to pay, pay supplier cash) but it is expensive; it is money tied up not directly earning a return – hence it will decrease profitability, not increase it.

Statement 3 is correct. Too much or too little working capital leads to poor business performance. Too much reduces profitability, too little is risky. Hence managing it to an appropriate level is important for a business if it is to be successful.

Statement 4 is incorrect. The two objectives of working capital management are to ensure the business has sufficient liquid resources and increase profitability. These objectives will often conflict as liquid assets give the lowest returns.

60   The correct answer is: Statement 2 only

Statement 2 relates to an aggressive approach to financing working capital while statement 1 relates to a conservative approach to financing working capital.